Part One
Dostoevsky
1

Russia geographically is so huge that something inside a Russian feels without limit. No matter how strongly Russians are controlled politically, they still feel that something within them, some sense of themselves that arises freely in their souls, can never be controlled. The soul cries out that it should not be ruled by anything, neither by a power in the outside world nor by some power in the mind. At times something wonderful comes alive in the Russian soul, something infinitely gentle and unworldly. Even when such moments pass, Russians refuse to believe their souls are empty and worthless. This belief gives the soul the strength to endure anything coming at it from the outside world.

Western European values based on materialism and scientific rationality entered Russia in the 18th century. They did not fit smoothly with Russian customs. Tsar Peter the Great imported Italian and French artists and architects to build the city of Saint Petersburg using eighteenth-century technologies. The result was a strange artificial city placed on Russian soil as if from nowhere. Fyodor Dostoevsky, the nineteenth-century Russian novelist, wrote that the Tsar's city, Saint Petersburg, is "the most abstract and intentional city on the whole terrestrial globe". The idea that a city could be produced intentionally stuck in Dostoevsky's mind. If a whole city resulted from a premeditated rational idea, what prevented people in an intentional city from acting intentionally? And if architects could create a city intentionally, why could not he, Dostoevsky, create a novel with a hero who acts only intentionally and refuses to act naturally like those around him?

Let's follow his young intentional hero through the streets of Saint Petersburg in the 1860s. Where is the young man, Raskolnikov, going? He is on his way to visit a sixty-year-old woman, a pawnbroker. He has visited her before and pawned objects for money. He is dressed negligently and is in need of money. He lives in a very small room, has little means and is thin and poorly nourished. He enters the woman's apartment and talks with her about how much money she will give him for a watch.

She gives him one rouble and fifteen kopecks but money this day is not his only object. Raskolnikov intends to experiment intentionally with reality rather than let reality experiment with him as do most people. He is going to test Western European rationalistic culture. Such culture exists inside him because he is perfectly capable as are other Petersburg students of acting rationally. It is in fact the easiest thing in the world to be rational and act rationally but something urges him to carry rationality to an extreme, to test how far rationality can go.

Where did Saint Petersburg come from? Why is Tzar Peter the Great's "intentional" city here? Where is the spiritual freedom and cultural independence of the Russian past? Why are some people around him as he walks to the pawnbroker dressed in Western European style clothes? Don't they see that they look odd compared to the way most people in Petersburg dress? He too when he dresses well is peculiar just like they. And all the socialist agitators in his neighborhood, don't they realize that their ideas are unseemly, that their revolutionary desire to create some new world is illusory? Raskolnikov is going to find out if an action motivated by nothing at all except a rational intention born in his own mind and nowhere else can be authentic. Why should not a rational person, if he must live guided by his reason because he lives in a modern abstract and intentional city, not be allowed to do anything at all that can be conceived rationally? A rational being like young Raskolnikov might act rationally in order to do something that the masses of people think despicable, evil, insane, but could not a man superior to the masses prove his superiority by daring to do something of the sort? He might use his reason to the extreme to establish his superiority just as the rational Western European architects went to a rational extreme by constructing Peter the Great's "intentional" city. If rationality is the final destiny of all humans, something they must adopt to conduct their lives whether they like it or not, if rationality is everything then everything must be able to be done rationally, and even an insane terrible act should not have an irrational result in a feeling of guilt or shame if it is done intentionally. Raskolnikov has been alone brooding and thinking in his small room for many days avoiding human contact. He visits the pawnbroker not just for money but also to examine the inside of her apartment. One idea dominates his being, the idea of slicing an axe into the skull of the old pawnbroker simply to prove to himself that he could carry out rationally any act no matter how terrible.

Dostoevsky knew that Russian holy men of God are not motivated by the mind but by feelings that come from the heart. But why could he not create a new opposite type of holy man, a sort of holy man in reverse, a man who dares to draw his inspiration not from the feelings within his heart but from the ideas in his mind? Raskolnikov wants to use his mind to go beyond the normal mind. His mind and his self have become the same thing. He does not want to have anything to do with feelings of any kind. The miserable people around him on the streets of Petersburg are full of feelings because in their misery they have no tool to try to escape from their poverty except their feelings which are petty and inspired by their misery and just lead to more misery. Raskolnikov is a creature of bourgeois culture living in his mind and willing to test his mind to the extreme to experience its limitless power. Dostoevsky's ultimate message in his novel *Crime And Punishment* is that to live guided by ideas alone turns you yourself into a kind of abstract being that is no longer your true being. The living soul within you becomes a thing if you become instead of a living human being an idea directing the way you act.

Yet as Raskolnikov walks along the street in Petersburg after his meeting with the old pawnbroker, he feels the need for human contact. He has been alone for many days in his little shabby room avoiding contact with people, living in his mind forgetful of normal life. He comes to the entrance to a cheap tavern and decides to go in and drink a beer. He is a young handsome student whose mind has taken hold of him completely and driven him to try to live in a realm beyond that of normal people. But here in the tavern the side of himself that is normal comes to the surface and he feels "suddenly set free from a terrible burden". His burden, his problem is the power his mind exercises over his actions. A Russian critic of the 19th and 20th centuries, Lev Shestov, put the problem of living as an idea, Raskolnikov's problem, in this way, "Man does not dare or has no power to think in the categories in which he lives, and is forced to live in those categories in which he thinks." Raskolnikov has been living alone, estranged from society, living in the categories where he thinks. It is the problem of the Russian soul. A Russian wants to think only in the categories where he lives and he is horrified when something makes him live in the categories where he thinks. Raskolnikov's passion is to live always where he thinks and nowhere else but drinking his beer in the tavern he does escape for a time living where he thinks because he is among poor drunken common Russians who are incapable of doing anything but think where they live. Raskolnikov feels "suddenly set free from a terrible burden" but he also has "a dim foreboding that this happier frame of mind was...not normal". How long will he be free from his "terrible burden"? He will eventually have to leave his beer and his tavern and the world he faces outside will again make him think and thinking will again make him live in the categories where he thinks cut off from all regular human experience.

Dostoevsky's novel is just his fancy set down in words creating imagined humans in action. But the Russian problem of the soul is real and the problem Dostoevsky treats in his novel is real because it is a problem he never succeeded in solving by using his mind, by thinking. But he thought and thought and he thought like all of us and the more he thought the more he thought that the mind itself was the problem, or rather, that the mind could not ever solve the fundamental problem of Russia and of life. What to do? We must do something but to do something we must first think what we are going to do and then what we end up doing habitually transforms us and we soon become no longer our authentic self but some superficial self that our ego makes up for ourselves using the rational power of the mind. We give up our freedom and make ourselves objects so quickly and so normally and so automatically that we reach a point where we are not even aware that we have given up ourselves and become other than ourselves. This other alien self should be Raskolnikov's sworn enemy. But the enemy in his mind and in our minds is incapable of appearing to us as anything but our friend and we are afraid to think of him as an enemy from fear of perhaps going out of our minds. Raskolnikov is the kind of man who believes that something in the mind can reach out infinitely and discover something unknowable to the normal frame of mind. In some region of the mind, such men think, there is another dimension of the mind. The world is full of symbols of this transcendent world. All philosophers and scientists and some religious men believe this world, this other world, exists even though they never find it. But the quest for it is satisfying. It delights them that their petty human nature has a kind of divine globe, the mind, and they enjoy knowing that their minds give flashes at times of a world beyond our senses but not beyond our minds. No enemy lives within such men. They delight in thinking. Thinking leads to an absence of life that their ideas magically transform to the illusion of a presence. They think and think but it produces only more thinking not more life, not a release from the burden of life, but just more thinking until , as Lev Shestov wrote, they are not thinking in the categories where they live but living in the categories where they think.

In the tavern a man over fifty with a look in his eyes "as though of intense feeling" and perhaps "of thought and intelligence" but also with "a gleam of something like madness" begins talking to Raskolnikov. He moves to a seat at his table to engage him in conversation. He is dressed slovenly and is bloated with drink. He has been drinking for five days and sleeping on hay barges at night on the Neva river. His madness however is real. It is not at all like Raskolnikov's insanity of living as exclusively as possible in his mind. Marmeladov's madness comes from living blind to any thought about his welfare. He has given up everything. He is out of his mind because he has thrown away all interest in any thought that might lead him to some kind of normalcy by thinking and acting rationally. His madness is the kind of Russian madness that Dostoevsky loved. It is the kind that bravely throws overboard completely, as completely as possible, the regular rational thoughts of the mind. Dostoevsky loved such madness. Madness has driven Marmeladov to give up working and providing for his wife, three young children and a daughter of eighteen. Instead he uses what money they might have used to ease their starvation for drink. Living only where you think, or at least living as best you can where you think, is profitable. It is positive. It produces results. Marmeladov mentions, as he begins a long description for Raskolnikov of his sufferings, most of them caused by himself, that a certain Mr. Lebeziatnikov "who keeps up with modern ideas" explained to him the other day "that compassion is forbidden nowadays by science itself, and that that's what is done now in England, where there is political economy." Compassion is forbidden by science itself and this produces political economy. Political economy, science and rational behavior rule the world outside the tavern and produce positive results but inside the tavern in a world hidden from the ordinary world, what is truly alive is Marmeladov's madness, a madness that has its roots in the agony of remorse and human feelings caused by suffering.

Raskolnikov will carry out his idea. He will live ruled by an idea that will result in his murdering the old pawnbroker. His logic is that if one is forced to live where one thinks, then thought can produce an action totally devoid of human feeling. And if this is so, then even an extreme act like killing an old pawnbroker can be done without feeling. A human ruled completely by an extreme idea and willing to carry out the logic of his idea by a concrete action will become necessarily a human more than human, a superman. But testing this logic will happen in Raskolnikov's future. For the present, in our tavern, Marmeladov relates to Raskolnikov an act carried out by his young eighteen-year-old daughter Sonya not because of an idea but by compassion. Compassion, feeling, in the case of Sonya motivates the idea and then the act and not the other way around whereby some inhuman idea produces an act.

Sonya has once lived with Marmeladov and her stepmother, Katerina Ivanova, and her two stepbrothers and stepsister in one room in extreme poverty. They were starving because of Marmeladov's failings and in a rage caused by her extreme sufferings, Katerina Ivanova drove her pure and meek eighteen-year-old stepdaughter Sonya, who can find no legitimate work, to begin selling herself on the streets of Petersburg. In the tavern other men, listening to Marmeladov's conversation with Raskolnikov, laugh from time to time at what he relates. But when he speaks with deep feeling about what will be the ultimate fate of his daughter, strangely those listening are moved. But before we hear what Marmeladov says, inspired by religion, we should examine Dostoevsky's general point of view.

For Dostoevsky Raskolnikov, dressed carelessly, brooding alone day after day in his room barely bigger than a closet, eating little, avoiding human contact, despising the life going on around him, is a pastiche, carried to an absurd degree, of an eastern holy man. He wants to go beyond the life around him by using his mind so exclusively that he loses touch with regular life. He denies life to find life like some eastern holy man and this direction for Dostoevsky leads to nothing, to a transcendence of normal life that is empty and worthless and destructive. For Dostoevsky, all of Western European culture goes in this direction. The mind dictates in Europe how life should be lived. It is the source of truth and goodness. Even refined poetic and aesthetic experience is fashioned into cultural objects by the mind and all scientific and mathematical products are always the result of rational thinking. The Western European ideal of blessedness is the state of the perfectly indifferent mind thinking about itself. Thinkers like Aristotle and Plato and others in the ancient world along with medieval European scholastic thinkers of the Catholic Church as well as renaissance thinkers down to the rule in Dostoevsky's time of European thinkers who exclude experience that does not fit within the boundaries of bourgeois rationalism have fallen all of them into the mind's fatal trap. European thought has led Europeans to live in the categories where they think. Dostoevsky will have none of it. For him Raskolnikov is searching for a separate superior state of being that does not exist except as an illusion created by the power of his mind. Only Marmeladov's madness can lead to real spirituality because it is profoundly human.

At this point in his novel Dostoevsky throws out to us bits of Christian religious truth as an example of truth totally beyond the vision and the soul of his main character, Raskolnikov. He knows that we as well as Raskolnikov will pay no attention to what Marmeladov says. We all live in the categories where we think and we are too fascinated, as we read along, with young Raskolnikov's adventure inspired by his mind. It is where we ourselves look too for adventure and we pass quickly over what Marmeladov says. It is the raving of a madman. It has nothing to do with rational people like Raskolnikov and ourselves.

Marmeladov's daughter Sonya has gone out to the streets to earn money to feed her stepmother and her stepbrothers and stepsister. She even is so humble and self-sacrificing that she gives some of the money so fouly earned to her father to continue his five-day drunk. "He will pity us Who has had pity on all men," Marmeladov says with genuine human feeling to young Raskolnikov sitting across the table in the tavern listening. "He will come in that day and he will ask: 'Where is the daughter who gave herself for her cross, consumptive stepmother, and for the little children of another? Where is the daughter who had pity on the filthy drunkard, her earthly father, undismayed by his beastliness?' And He will say, 'Come to me! I have already forgiven thee once...I have forgiven thee once... Thy sins which are many are forgiven thee for thou hast loved much...' And he will forgive my Sonya, He will forgive, I know it...I felt it in my heart when I was with her just now!" But Dostoevsky does not end Marmeladov's passionate words here. He does not let those who live by rationality and without compassion and have achieved "political economy" slip away without throwing them a punch. For as he continues his passionate outpouring of his feelings Marmeladov speaks of what will be said at the final judgment to "the wise ones and those of understanding" and he explains why the meek and the humble and weak will be accepted by Him. "This is why I receive them, o ye wise," Marmeladov goes on with feeling, "this is why I receive them, o ye of understanding, that not one of them believed himself to be worthy of this."

Two days later, Raskolnikov will hammer the blunt backside of an axe onto the head of a sixty-year-old woman, a pawnbroker, killing her. A few moments after the murder, while he searches in the dead woman's bedroom for valuables, the pawnbroker's half-sister, Lizaveta, comes in the main room of the apartment and discovers the dead body of her half-sister on the floor bloodied. Raskolnikov already knows about Lizaveta and she knows a little about him from the comings and goings of people in that area of the city. Dostoevsky describes her, "She was a single woman of about thirty-five, tall, clumsy, timid, submissive and almost idiotic. She was a complete slave and went in fear and trembling of her sister, who made her work day and night, and even beat her." Lizaveta sees the dead body on the floor and then Raskolnikov comes out of the bedroom. "And this hapless Lizaveta was so simple and had been so thoroughly crushed and scared that she did not even raise a hand to guard her face, though that was the most necessary and natural action at the moment, for the axe was raised above her face. She only put up her empty left hand, but not to her face, slowly holding it out before her as though motioning him away. The axe fell with the sharp edge just on the skull and split at one blow all the top of the head."

2

What can be done with such people? Isn't the logic directing Raskolnikov's act reasonable? Does an old woman, a pawnbroker scratching out a living for herself on the poverty and misery of the poor, deserve to live? Of course everyone knows what is evil and what is good and she should absolutely not be murdered with a blow on her head from an axe, but isn't it more or less necessary to murder her some way or another? What role can she play in society except to live a miserable life? Isn't misery itself a kind of murder, a slow murder of the poor by those who possess riches and live a higher form of life enlightened by reason? And the hapless Lizaveta, simple and meek and crushed by the burden of living, what can society do with her except find some way to get rid of her, not murder her but at least keep her out of sight somewhere so that enlightened people don't come in contact with her disgraceful poverty? Besides, it was an accident that caused her death. She happened to walk into the scene of her half-sister's murder and confront by accident her killer. Raskolnikov was forced by circumstances to kill her too. Circumstances and chance kill the poor all the time. To be unlucky is disgraceful and all the poor are unlucky. They are incapable of living rationally, of making real progress. They don't think in the proper manner about their actions before they take action. They deserve their fate. In fact, from a larger point of view, the poor are necessary in order to give higher meaning to the lives of the rich and successful. The enlightenment of the mind is a necessary development that superior people seek caused partly by their observation of the miserable lives of the poor. Raskolnikov is an instrument of bourgeois society. He took a drastic step upward to enlightenment by ridding society of two beings whom society in a civilized manner was getting rid of anyway.

The only thing Raskolnikov cares about after the double murder is himself. Two men come to the door of the pawnbroker's apartment. When the bell of the apartment tinkles and then someone begins banging loudly on the door, he has no thought at all of the two dead women near him on the floor. A giddiness comes over him but when a voice on the other side of the door calls out loudly to the pawnbroker, he recovers himself. He thinks and thinks and thinks again of how to escape. He sneaks out to the street unobserved aided by his reason now alive and vital and dynamic. It has become a strange delight for him to now exist safely only by thinking and to be isolated now in a state of supreme detachment from any connection with people he now passes on the street. He is no longer like those around him. He alone counts. His safety, his defiance of all regular habits, his criminal state, this alone now makes Raskolnikov Raskolnikov.

At any moment society can reach out and grasp him like some scared chicken running around a farmyard unless he pretends successfully to be like everyone else. Only his mind is of any use in this new exhilarating drama. He must make himself as enlightened as possible. He is like an actor in a theater separated from the public before him and feeling strangely and magically alive even though his every word and his every act is counterfeited and false. He must be a light shining in the darkness of a society now totally alien to him but a light visible only to himself. Remorse? It does not exist and can not exist in him because his state of criminality must have no influence at all coming from the soul if he is to exist successfully and safely. The problem of the Russian soul no longer exists for Raskolnikov. He is not divided anymore by the influences that drive the soul inwardly or outwardly. He is condemned by his criminal act to live only where he thinks and it excites him to live there with a strange delight that grows more delightful as he escapes again and again from normal humans who are all now his enemies.

Raskolnikov has now reached, in a strange and unique fashion, the pinnacle of Western European religious and intellectual culture. His mind produced the thoughts that led to his crime but it observed his crime with perfect indifference just as it does all human actions. He can no longer live ever again as a normal human unless the unthinkable happens and he breaks the connection with his mind that his thinking produces. In order to experience remorse for what he has done, he would have to reach a place in his soul where a mysterious voice that has nothing to do with his mind and his thoughts cries out to him passionately *that he should not have done it.* This is impossible. Remorse is a form of compassion, a kind of compassion that a person feels for himself, a compassion of regret for a wrong he has committed. Modern European science, according to what a man has told Marmeladov, forbids compassion and successful enlightened modern Europeans have forbidden themselves not only compassion but remorse for the sufferings and injuries they inflict on the poor. Dostoevsky resists any attempt on his part to direct his hero towards remorse and instead directs him to imprison himself in his own mind more and more intensely even when influences caused by compassion for him by others should move him towards remorse. Dostoevsky is not out to convert Raskolnikov to the truths of the soul. He has driven Raskolnikov's self so deeply into his mind that there is no place within him anymore for a soul. He does have moments when he is moved by compassion for the poor and he has other emotional moments, especially moments of fear, but these are fleeting moments.

But not all Western Europeans of Dostoevsky's time were without compassion for the poor. The best of the

Europeans were against modern bourgeois capitalist culture, as was Dostoevsky, but Dostoevsky by the time he wrote of Raskolnikov had abandoned the solution Europeans had found for the problem, socialism. They had really no answer for the sufferings of "the people" driven to poverty and despair by the bourgeoisie except some new form of society that would force all to become brotherly by working together collectively for common economic benefits. Dostoevsky grew to despise modern Europeans and their modern culture based exclusively on rationality and selfishness. He never ceases throughout his works to invent odd characters like Raskolnikov who have evolved into strange aberrations from everything normal in life except that they usually do not abandon rationality but instead transform it to new, strange expressions. Many of the European socialists saw clearly as did Dostoevsky the decadence of late-nineteenth-century capitalism, but Dostoevsky had given up the socialistic views of his youth and grew to hate all liberal and socialist based thoughts designed to solve Russia's suffering.

Dostoevsky had been a member of a radical group when he was twenty-seven that was inspired by liberal and socialist ideas. Some members of the group met secretly, obtained a printing press, and planned to publish their radical notions for changing society for the better. Dostoevsky was arrested along with others and condemned by the government to be shot by a firing squad. The young writer stood on a platform on a cold December morning waiting for the bullets that would end all his radical thoughts and along with them all his regular human thoughts of whatever kind forever. In those seconds before his death Dostoevsky, to borrow Lev Shestov's expression, received "a new pair of eyes". Never again after he received his new eyes, both during the few seconds that remained to him before his death and in the millions of seconds that remained to him because the Tsar unexpectedly stopped his execution — — never again did he look at anything only with regular, normal eyes. But what changed the sight that came forth from his eyes was what the nearness of death had done to his soul. He would never again look at anything except with the new vision that the eyes of the soul gave him. We can not know ourselves what he experienced in those deadly seconds when his death was certain and about to arrive instantly and certainly. We see it with our normal eyes but our eyes are guided by our minds and not by our soul so we do not see what Dostoevsky suddenly saw and continued to see. We think he gained his new eyes because of some kind of religious experience and since we think of religion as being something above and beyond our normal life, we think that Dostoevsky must have begun looking beyond his merely human life to something divine and spiritual in some hidden world above and beyond the human world. Dostoevsky was a Christian but his Christianity did not change his purely human actions and instead taught him he should not change, that his human nature itself, insulted, injured and suffering, was the only temple in which the true God could be met truly. All types of religious experience that were based on seeking some divine experience achieved through some type of mental discipline became alien to him. He grew to hate all doctrines that tried to separate a human being from his authentic self. Liberal ideas, socialist ideas, even some Christian ideas — — he threw them all away onto the same garbage heap where the experience of facing death had thrown away his old eyes. He despised all Western

European thought because it was all based on elevated forms of reasoning that did little more than alienate a human being from his own being. European critics experienced his despite and contempt for them and lashed back at him. The German bourgeois novelist Thomas Mann said that Dostoevsky's works were full of "religious prating". A Russian critic despised him as someone always "looking for buried treasure". In his greatest novel, *The Possessed*, he creates a character, based on the Russian writer Turgenev, and makes him the butt of his satire almost maliciously. Turgenev in turn despised Dostoevsky's Christianity and gave an example of the cruel beating he observed him once giving his servant as illustrating the effect on Dostoevsky of his Christianity. Turgenev believed Dostoevsky was a writer who knew nothing of real freedom, which for Turgenev was based, as among all Western European intellectuals, on the elevating power of the mind. What interested Dostoevsky most was not religion itself, or doctrines of any kind including even Christian doctrine, but humans driven to the point where they might change radically and discover not some divine world off somewhere in the clouds but the new self within them, rooted in their very humanity, that they themselves had been themselves hiding from themselves. The mind made men and women selfish and cruel humans yet Dostoevsky sought God paradoxically only in humans and nowhere else.

Raskolnikov is a holy man in reverse, that is, for Dostoevsky he is not a holy man at all and until he has himself discovered that his human nature when ruled only by the mind is foul, he will never be anything, nothing but a human nothing living in the categories where he thinks. He goes out of his little room a short time after his crime thinking not of the murders but only of walking about and finding some place to get rid of the objects he possesses taken from the pawnbroker that might be evidence of his involvement. He buries them under a huge stone. Then he walks on without resting. "He had a terrible longing for some distraction, but he did not know what to do, what to attempt. A new overwhelming sensation was gaining more and more mastery over him every moment; this was an immeasurable, almost physical, repulsion for everything surrounding him, an obstinate, malignant feeling of hatred. All who met him were loathsome to him — he loathed their faces, their movements, their gestures. If anyone had addressed him, he felt that he might have spat at him or bitten him…"

Who is mad, Marmeladov or Raskolnikov? If they are both mad then they are mad in two different ways completely. Before the murders just after the talk between Raskolnikov and Marmeladov in the tavern, we get a closer look at Marmeladov's type of madness. It is profoundly human. The two leave the tavern and Raskolnikov aids the older, drunken man to walk home. Instead of walking into his one-room home with three starving children and his emaciated, sickly wife, Katerina Ivanova, Marmeladov drops to his knees in the doorway. "'Ah!,' she cried out in a frenzy, 'he has come back! The criminal! The monster!…And where is the money? What's in your pocket, show me! And your clothes are all different! Where are your clothes? Where is the money! Speak!'" All the money is gone. "She seized him by the hair and dragged him into the room. Marmeladov seconded her efforts by meekly crawling along on his knees." Marmeladov's madness separated him from his family but not by any means from human feeling and he returned to his family to remain with it full of remorse. Raskolnikov's madness is purely of the mind so it is not Marmeladov's kind of madness. It is a separation from human feeling. It is the doctrine of self-isolation taught by the mind whenever an ego submits to it that it wants to be nothing but an ego more powerful than all other egos, an ego that can not see with the eyes of a Dostoevsky that see that such an ego imprisoned by such a mind is worthless.

3

After the murder and after hiding the stolen objects, Raskolnikov returns to his small room. He is in a kind of delirium for five days, eating little, sleeping for long periods. His friend, the student Razumihin, looks over him and the servant girl in his rooming house, Nastasya, looks in on him at times offering food or tea. Razumihin informs him during one of his awakened periods that money has arrived from his mother and sister who will soon arrive in Petersburg. Razumihin, a young healthy positive type, uses the money to buy Raskolnikov a new set of clothes and he has brought to his room an acquaintance, the doctor Zossimov, to look over him. Raskolnikov treats them indifferently, even spitefully, paying little attention to them. Only when they start discussing the murders does Raskolnikov revive and give them his full attention. Pyotr Petrovitch Luzhin, a successful government official, arrives to present himself to Raskolnikov. He has recently become engaged to Raskolnikov's sister. He is a forty-five-year-old positive figure. Raskolnikov has found out through a letter sent to him by his mother just before the murders that his young sister has accepted Luzhin's proposal of marriage only to gain a higher more secure place in society for her mother and her brother Raskolnikov whom she loves dearly. Razumihin and

Zossimov treat Luzhin respectfully, agreeing in their conversation with some of Luzhin's liberal ideas. Raskolnikov accuses Luzhin, breaking in on the conversation, of putting his mother and sister up in a cheap boarding house in Petersburg. Worse still, influenced by what his mother has reported of what Luzhin said during his courtship, Raskolnikov again breaks in on the conversation. "'And is it true,' Raskolnikov asked Luzhin, in a voice quivering with fury and delight in insulting him, 'is it true that you told your *fiancee*...within an hour of her acceptance, that what pleased you most...was that she was a beggar...because it was better to raise a wife from poverty, so that you may have complete control over her, and reproach her with your being her benefactor?'" After defending himself with some embarrassment, the insult soon drives Luzhin from Raskolnikov's little room"How could you — how could you!" Razumihin says to Raskolnikov just after Luzhin leaves, "shaking his head in perplexity".

"'Let me alone — let me alone all of you!' Raskolnikov cried in a frenzy. 'Will you ever leave off tormenting me? I am not afraid of you! I am not afraid of anyone, anyone now! Get away from me. I want to be alone, alone, alone!'"

Razumihin and Zossimov leave at once but strangely Raskolnikov left alone does not remain in his room alone. His defense of his sister with his stinging insult to the man she is engaged to marry is the first genuinely human experience he has had since the murders and it perhaps motivates him to leave his room and seek some contact with the world outside of his room and his mind. Dostoevsky must bring his character into the everyday world of normal men and women if he is to somehow bring him also towards the world of human remorse which is never discovered in the human mind relying only on itself for guidance.

He dresses in his new set of clothes that Razumihin has bought for him, puts his rubles and his kopecks in his pocket, and steps out into the Petersburg night. It is eight o'clock with the sun setting and he does not think where he is going. Thought now, for some reason, tortures him. He now feels "that everything must be changed 'one way or another'". We have suddenly left thought, the world of thought, and have begun taking steps towards the world of feeling. He walks toward the Hay Market. He comes to a young man with a barrel organ accompanying the singing of a girl of fifteen hoping to earn a few kopecks. Raskolnikov stops and listens among two or three listeners. He takes out a five kopeck piece and puts it in the girl's hand. He is on the street and among people and the man who sliced an axe onto the head of Lizaveta who "only put up her empty left hand" touches the hand of a girl. It is a sign, a brief sign from Dostoevsky, that his character has taken the first step to the only world that counts because it is the only world that is real, the human world. Dostoevsky will never read any sign, any of the thousands of signs in the universe without and in the mind within, that lead anywhere "upward" and "beyond" mentally or physically, spiritually or scientifically. He will follow no sign unless it leads to a purely human step.

A middle-aged man is standing idly by Raskolnikov as they listen to the boy and girl singing to music from a street organ. Raskolnikov tries for human contact with a stranger. " 'I love to hear singing to a street organ,' said Raskolnikov, and his manner seemed strangely out of keeping with the subject. 'I like it on cold, dark, damp autumn evenings — they must be damp — when all the passers-by have pale green, sickly faces, or better still when wet snow is falling straight down, when there's no wind — you know what I mean? And the street lamps shine through it…'" "'I don't know…Excuse me', muttered the stranger, frightened by the question and Raskolnikov's strange manner, and he crossed over to the other side of the street."

Raskolnikov's manner is now strange in a way different from what it was before. Before his manner was strange because of his silence and his need to be separate from people around him. Now his manner is strange because of the way he talks to people in his surroundings. His need to talk seems like perhaps the first steps from his former silent madness ruled by his mind towards the Marmeladov kind of madness that has its origin in human feeling. But in Dostoevsky's understanding of psychology, the mind and the soul are enemies and neither show any mercy to the other until one gives in to the other and commits itself because of its defeat to be the other's servant. Raskolnikov has felt a minor touch of compassion and pressed five kopecks into the hand of a girl. He has sent off words of feeling and poetry to the astonished ears of a stranger. Something is making him speak. What if this something continues to put pressure on him? What if it presses him not to just talk but to talk about it? He had but one thought earlier when he left his room. His complete thought was "that all *this* must be ended today, once for all, immediately; that he would not return home without it, because he *would not go on living like that.*" Raskolnikov like Marmeladov has now a need to get everything out in the open.

His wanderings this night through the Hay Market and other places around Petersburg where normal people are doing normal things trying to enjoy the evening include a series of accidents. He tries to get information from hucksters in the Hay Market who had dealings with Lizaveta. He speaks to a young man standing before a shop. But he makes no progress with his questions. The young man quickly tires of talking to him and directs him laughing to an eating-house saying "you'll find princesses there too....La,la". He crosses a square and pushes his way into a dense crowd of peasants. "He felt an unaccountable inclination to enter into conversation with people. But the peasants took no notice of him; they were all shouting in groups together." He wandered off silently to a marketplace that he knew well with dram shops and eating-houses. He saw women running in and out of various festive establishments. From one came the sounds of singing, the tinkling of a guitar and shouts of merriment. He passed a drunken soldier swearing and smoking a cigarette. A beggar was quarrelling with another beggar and a drunk was lying right across the road. Life, in other words, the bald unthinking life of real people, humans, is all around him. He is now in the midst of life unfolding not intentionally but accidentally. Two women speak to him seductively. One asks him for six kopecks for a drink and he gives her fifteen. A woman "pock-marked...covered with bruises with her upper lip swollen" but nonetheless alive and, so to speak, greedy to continue living to her last breath sets Raskolnikov to thinking about life. "'Where is it,' thought Raskolnikov. 'Where is it I've read that someone condemned to death says or thinks, an hour before his death, that if he had to live on some high rock, on such a narrow ledge that he'd have only the room to stand, and the ocean, everlasting darkness, everlasting solitude, everlasting tempest around him, if he had to remain standing on a square yard of space all his life, a thousand years, eternity, it were better to live so than to die at once! Only to live, to live and live! Life, whatever it may be!'" But Raskolnikov is still thinking not living and his thinking has him in such a firm grip that it will not allow him to live like those around him.

He remembers why he has come out, to get some newspapers to read what has been written about the murders. He enters a spacious and clean restaurant and orders tea and newspapers. Suddenly, as he searches the newspapers, the head clerk of the police station that he has recently visited on a matter not related to the murders, sits down smiling at his table. Zametov tells him that he has visited him recently at his room when he was lying on his couch sleeping. Raskolnikov talks to him strangely and insultingly. He accuses him of drinking champagne at others expense. He accuses him of taking money corruptly and profiting from everything. Zametov has sat down for friendly conversation and tells Raskolnikov he is speaking strangely and must still be unwell. The conversation goes on back and forth argumentatively with no normal human connection between the murderer and the police official. They begin on the subject that Raskolnikov has just been reading about in the newspapers, the murders of the two women. Raskolnikov gives a long description of what he would have done if he were the murderer to hide the objects that were stolen from the dead pawnbroker. But he describes to Zametov in great detail how he actually hid the objects under a stone without admitting to Zametov that he was the murderer and as though he were simply imagining for Zametov's benefit how he would have hidden the objects. Zametov calls him a madman because he is fed up with Raskolnikov's wild, strange imaginings. "'And what if it was I who murdered the old woman and Lizaveta?' he said suddenly and — realized what he had done." Zametov decides Raskolnikov is merely joking or playing with him maliciously and refuses to believe him. But Raskolnikov has really said it! He has gotten the truth in his mind out in the company of men! It jolts him and he soon leaves the restaurant. "He went out, trembling all over from a sort of wild hysterical sensation, in which there was an element of insufferable rapture." But this touch of sudden, intense life comes from a daring intentional act of the mind not from a sudden touch of remorse in the soul.

4

A series of accidents happen to Raskolnikov but his behavior is so intentional, intentional to the extreme, that when he sees evidence that a young girl, Sonya, the daughter of Marmeladov, possesses something infinitely gentle and unworldly in her soul, some hidden spiritual power that protects her from the world around her — — even when Raskolnikov sees clearly that such a spirit lives within her and he also understands that because of what is in her soul he himself is permanently joined to the young woman forever, even at such a moment that has all the appearance of a miracle, it does not affect his feelings because his rational madness, even in the face of a miracle, will not let him set his soul free.

Raskolnikov's meeting with Marmeladov in a tavern after his visit to the old pawnbroker was the first accident. They do not know each other, yet Marmeladov is moved somehow to talk to young Raskolnikov and pour out his remorseful feelings to him without any restraint. We accept it as a reasonably possible occurrence because Raskolnikov is a completely believable character, an intelligent young student pursuing some odd adventure. Marmeladov's ravings present us with a nice contrast to Raskolnikov's rationality to such an extent that we do not hear with any feeling the odd things the father says about his daughter Sonya who has been driven to prostitution by her miserable poverty. Yet what a superb accident it is to set a young man soon to become an axe murderer of two women at the same table in a dismal tavern with a madman! The religious language Marmeladov uses appears to us to be nonsense. The concrete belief he expresses, that his daughter Sonya's sins will be forgiven, is nonsense and the absurd reasoning he uses to explain why Sonya will be saved is nonsense carried to the extreme. Sonya will be saved because she has "loved much". It is such nonsense that our minds do not allow us to see that something has already slipped secretly into Raskolnikov's soul and our souls. Love! But we do not feel this love and our minds automatically reject it as nonsense. Marmeladov does feel it but he is nothing but a madman. His dear daughter is on the streets prostituting herself and he dares to say that she will be forgiven because she has loved! "Thy sins which are many," Marmeladov raves, "are forgiven thee for thou hast loved much." We are happy when the scene moves on and we are past such nonsense about the power of "love". We must soon also hear mad talk from Marmeladov of people, drunkards, "made in the image of the beast", who will be received into Christ's kingdom, not because they love but because "not one of them believed himself to be worthy of this". It is all nonsense that serves only as a nice contrast to the refined rational madness of Raskolnikov. We do not look for any new development of "love" in our story because it is about murder.

The next accident is that Marmeladov is so weakened and so drunk that he can not walk home unassisted. Raskolnikov is thus diverted from his extreme adventure of the mind by the practical job of helping his new acquaintance home. Because of his help, he finds out accidentally the address of Marmeladov's family and even enters the room where his wife and three stepchildren live. Sonya, Marmeladov's daughter, is not there and there seems little chance that Raskolnikov will ever meet her since she lives in another residence. He leaves on a window unnoticed the last few kopecks he has in his pockets for the starving family. On the stairs as he leaves the building, he regrets leaving the money thinking of the absent Sonya and her profession. He thinks not of how she will be saved by love but instead that money earned by her profession will provide food for her family and that leaving her family his last kopecks was stupid.

Later, after his five days spent in his room sleeping and in a delirium, when Raskolnikov puts on his new set of clothes and goes out walking through Petersburg at night, he is no longer acting as intentionally as a murderer should. His talk with people in the street is loose and unordinary. When he blurts out to the police clerk Zametov in the restaurant, "And what if it was I who murdered the old woman and Lizaveta?" he reveals that he is not fully in control of himself. He is now accident prone. As he leaves the restaurant, he "stumbled against Razumihin on the steps. They did not see each other till they almost knocked against one another." He does not want to be with his friend. They talk back and forth and he breaks free from his company. He stops on a bridge and while looking at the setting sun and the dark water of the river, he accidentally views an intentional act of a woman in despair. She jumps off the bridge. She is pulled out of the water but Raskolnikov looks on "with a strange sense of indifference and apathy. He felt disgusted." He leaves the river and walks towards the police station to "make an end" but on his way, he "turned into a side street and went two streets out of his way, possibly without any object, or possibly to delay a minute and gain time." This accidental or intentional change of direction takes him to "the very gate of *the* house". He goes in and up to the fourth floor and enters again the apartment, the scene of the crime. Does he return accidentally or intentionally? It is difficult to say but in any case it is a nice play between the accidental and the intentional if he returns by accident to the place of the murder that he committed intentionally. However when he leaves the house, he does have a very clear intention "for he had fully made up his mind to go to the police station and knew that it would all soon be over". But on his way, he sees a crowd forming and went up to it. There has been an accident!

An accident that brings him once again accidentally into the world of the madman Marmeladov. A carriage has run over him. Only Raskolnikov knows his identity and his address. Marmeladov is so extremely wounded that Raskolnikov urges the police to call for a doctor and help him carry the injured man who is near death to his residence that is nearby. He shouts that he will pay the expenses. At the room of his wife, Katerina Ivanova, it is revealed by the doctor who examines Marmeladov that there is no hope. Marmeladov dies ten minutes later. His wife has sent her daughter Polenka, a child of eleven, to run to her stepsister's residence. Marmeladov's daughter

Sonya arrives. Her father is able to raise himself up a little and beg her forgiveness. He dies embracing her. Raskolnikov confesses to Katerina Ivanova that Marmeladov was his friend. He gives the impoverished widow all the money he has, twenty roubles, and leaves.

The appearance of Sonya, "a small thin girl of eighteen with fair hair, rather pretty, with wonderful blue eyes" is a miracle. Or rather, her accidental appearance in Raskolnikov's life gives him the opportunity, as we will see, of perceiving later when he gets to know her that a miracle, a miraculous indescribable *something* lives within her that is a source to her of divine strength. For the present however she does communicate something to Raskolnikov by her unexpected action that touches him deeply, something that can be described truly, given the absurd rational intentionality of our axe murderer, as a miraculous influence. As Raskolnikov is leaving the building and on the last steps, Polenka, the eleven-year-old stepsister of Sonya, calls after him to wait. Sonya has sent her after him to find out his name and where he lives."Who sent you?" asks Raskolnikov. "'Sister Sonya sent me,' answered the girl, smiling...brightly." "I knew it was sister Sonya sent you," says Raskolnikov. "Mamma sent me too…when sister Sonya was sending me, mamma came up too and said, 'Run fast, Polenka'" "Do you love sister Sonya?" asks Raskolnikov. " 'I love her more than anyone,' Polenka answered with a peculiar earnestness, and her smile became graver." "And will you love me?", asks Raskolnikov.

A series of accidents has led an axe murderer, the murderer of Lizaveta who raised only one hand up as he was about to slice his axe into her head, to ask a child to love him. He certainly does not deserve her love but he receives it anyway in spite of what he has done: that is what makes it miraculous.

"By way of answer he saw the little girl's face approaching him, her full lips naively held out to kiss him. Suddenly her arms as thin as sticks held him tightly, her head rested on his shoulder and the little girl wept softly, pressing her face against him."

Sonya has sent a little angel to Raskolnikov and we will see that, despite her foul profession, Sonya is a divine woman or at least a woman whose soul is permanently influenced by something divine. But we should be careful and not begin thinking that Dostoevsky is out to show us angels or divine women as symbols of a divine world beyond and above us. He is not after some divine world up in the clouds. He is after what is inside humans and only what is truly inside them, holy or unholy. He has no eyes to look into the souls of people like Raskolnikov's sister's fiance, Luzhin, or bourgeois rational people in general because they have covered themselves over with layer after layer of stuffed-shirt rationalism and intentional behavior. They don't look ever into their own souls and have condemned themselves to being soulless. But people like Sonya, degraded and humiliated by her poverty, defenseless, have nothing at all coming from the outside world or coming from what is superficial in their own nature to help them construct some kind of strong practical ego. Everything around them insults their nature and makes them suffer. They can be looked into by Dostoevsky because they have nothing left to give themselves except their soul. He is not against angels and saints but he is not interested in them. He is passionate about trying to see if there is anything divine on earth and he knows for certain that if there is it can only be found in the human soul, a place that accidentally became visible to him when the Tsar of all the Russians cancelled at the last moment his execution and gave him a second pair of eyes.

5

During a scene at Raskolnikov's room between his friend, Razumihin, his sister Dounia, and his mother, Pulcheria Alexandrovna, Sonya opens the door and walks in. She has come to invite Raskolnikov to her father's funeral and also to the dinner her stepmother is preparing that will take place after the burial. She is extremely embarrassed and her child-like "kindliness and simplicity in her expression" touches Raskolnikov. Sonya is also touched by him. He asks her for her address and promises to come to see her. Her appearance in the room of the murderer is angelic and something passes between the two that comes into Raskolnikov's soul from a world that for him does not exist. She in turn feels a mysterious connection with Raskolnikov. "Never, never had she felt anything like this. Dimly and unconsciously a whole new world was opening before her." When Raskolnikov comes to her residence later the same day, he has a long talk with the angelic Sonya and has a chance to enter this "whole new world" that has opened before Sonya. Something during this their second meeting attaches him permanently to her but something else prevents him from entering her world.

It is a main theme of Dostoevsky's novels to bring characters struggling mightily with mental problems of various kinds to the point of belief. But most of them never make a magical leap of faith. What blocks them for the most part is an extreme reliance on the power of the mind although the influence of their mind does not completely explain their inability to reach the baptism that awaits them by a discovery of an independent, blessed power in their soul. Their isolation in their minds is strange, mysterious. An interesting way to understand the direction that Dostoevsky's characters take is to compare them with the direction of Shakespeare's Hamlet. Hamlet at the beginning of the play is an emotional mystic who talks to a ghost, the supposed spirit of his dead father who urges him from somewhere beyond the grave to avenge his murder by his brother. Hamlet is unable to rely sufficiently on this mystical revelation to avenge his dead father by murdering his uncle. In fact, he does not know certainly, objectively that his uncle has murdered his father until the third act. Finally, at the end of the play, Hamlet's development leads him to rely solely on his rationality to direct him. "Readiness is all", he announces in act five. Raskolnikov on the other hand is ready for all at the beginning of his drama and he never gives up his reliance on his reason. Hamlet's youthful madness at the beginning of the play when he talks to a spirit develops to a sane reliance on reason to keep him ready to face the world realistically. Raskolnikov develops from an extreme reliance on reason to an insane reliance on it. His development should be from the rational to the mystical, the very opposite of Hamlet's development, but, in the main body of his story, Dostoevsky will not allow him to go in that direction and discover the relief waiting for him in his soul. Raskolnikov's rational aberrations from the normal use of reason will be repeated often in other characters in other Dostoevsky novels taking other forms, but it is always the same theme and the same judgment on their author's part: an extreme reliance on reason alone becomes an insane aberration and drives a human completely away from any solace that can come to him from the soul. Sonya offers

Raskolnikov during their interview a way to reach down into his soul and drink the gentle waters of his soul's salvation but he does not go in the direction she offers.

In a dark room lit only by a candle, Sonya and Raskolnikov sit and talk. It is eleven at night. She is frightened by his unexpected visit at a late hour but happy to see him. He says that her stepmother, Katerina Ivanovna, used to beat her insinuating that the two have a bad relationship but Sonya explains that she loves her stepmother and that they are a close family. She expresses compassion for the sick woman with feeling as she speaks of the hardships of her life. Raskolnikov asks if she knew Lizaveta, the girl he murdered, and she answers that she did. As the talk goes on, he asks himself how she can live with such suffering, her own and her family's. He paces up and down the room thinking for five minutes in silence. "His eyes were hard, feverish and piercing, his lips were twitching. All at once he bent down quickly and dropping to the ground, kissed her foot." He explains that he has not bowed down to her but to "all the suffering of humanity". He says after a few moments that "your worst sin is that you have destroyed and betrayed yourself *for nothing*". He is now "almost in a frenzy". "Tell me how this shame and degradation can exist in you side by side with other, opposite, holy feelings?" It appears that he is going in the direction of the soul. He can not resist trying to know how she can be such a good person and live such a foul life. He cried to himself, "How can she sit on the edge of the abyss of loathsomeness into which she is slipping…? Does she expect a miracle?"

"'So you pray to God a great deal, Sonya?' he asked her.

Sonya did not speak; he stood beside her waiting for an

answer.

'What should I be without god?' she whispered rapidly, forcibly, glancing at him with suddenly flashing eyes, and squeezing his hand.

'Ah, so that is it!' he thought.

'And what does God do for you?' he asked, probing her further.

Sonya was silent for a long while, as though she could not answer. Her weak chest kept heaving with emotion.

'Be silent! Don't ask! You don't deserve!' she cried suddenly looking sternly and wrathfully at him.

'That's it, that's it,' he repeated to himself.

'He does everything,' she whispered quickly, looking down again."

The conflict is the same throughout most of Dostoevsky's works. It fascinates him to put side by side the angelic opposite the unholy, the good opposite the loathsome, faith opposite unbelief, the mystical opposite the rational. Usually there is somewhere a hint of a divine and miraculous world that flashes light very dimly towards his characters, a light that never quite reaches most of them, that never becomes a bright flash into their soul that might save them. Sonya is clearly an angel despite her profession and Raskolnikov is clearly a devil supported by the unrelenting power of the mind. They meet in a dark room lit only by a candle. Sonya's soul is bright with love. Raskolnikov's soul is a dark abyss and his mind a solid bridge above it.

Then a miracle takes place. Raskolnikov understands with his mind, objectively, that a secret divine presence is within Sonia. He accepts with his mind that God is alive within her protecting her even though he is unable or unwilling to jump across the gap between his mind and his soul, influenced by Sonya, to repent and to be saved. He asks himself, "What held her up — surely not depravity? All that infamy had obviously only touched her mechanically, not one drop of real depravity had penetrated to her heart; he saw that." He noticed a book on the top of a chest of drawers as he paced up and down the room. He picks it up and sees that it is a copy of the New Testament. She reveals that Lizaveta, the murdered young woman, brought it to her. He asks her to read the story of Lazarus whom Jesus raised from the dead. She hardly dares to read it to him because she says he does not believe but he insists and she reads. "Raskolnikov saw in part why Sonya could not bring herself to read to him and the more he saw this, the more roughly and irritably he insisted on her doing so. He understood only too well how painful it was for her to betray and unveil all that was her *own*. He understood that these feelings really were her *secret treasure,* which she had kept perhaps for years, perhaps from childhood, while she lived with an unhappy father and a distracted stepmother crazed by grief, in the midst of starving children and unseemly abuse and reproaches." He sees with the eyes of his mind inside Sonya's soul. He sees miraculously without feeling anything miraculous that a miracle is the source of her life, a hidden source.

She reads the whole story of the raising of Lazarus from the dead. In the night, in the dark room lit just by a candle, the murderer watches a saintly young girl reading "distinctly and forcibly as though she were making a public confession of faith". When she finishes her long reading, the two are silent in the dark room for five minutes. They have known one another since Marmeladov spoke of his daughter to Raskolnikov in the tavern saying passionately that her salvation is certain because she "has loved much" and they have been joined mysteriously since Sonya entered his room suddenly and angelically to invite him to attend her father's burial and her stepmother's reception, joined perhaps also when Sonya sent to him her stepsister Polenka with her childish love, and now joined forever because Raskolnikov has uncovered her secret strength, the divine love that lives in her soul, joined forever because now he has seen her faith as she read to him the story of Jesus raising Lazarus from death. But joined as they are they are also separated! It is a kind of miracle in reverse that Dostoevsky has invented. They are joined miraculously but at the same time they are adversaries. Raskolnikov will not move an inch from his imprisonment in his mind and believe. The truth is that he is so locked in the embrace of his mind that he is powerless to move to the other part of his being, the place where in Sonya's being she lives truly. But Sonya will not move an inch either. She accepts him as the partner of her life forever but never does she accept his condition of unbelief. A silent war goes on between the soul of one and the mind of the other.

Breaking the five minute silence, Raskolnikov confesses to her that he has broken completely with his family. "'I have only you now,' he added. 'Let us go together....I've come to you, we are both accursed, let us go our way together!'"

"'Go where?' she asked in alarm and she involuntarily stepped back." "'How do I know? I only know it's the same road, I know that and nothing more. It's the same goal!'"

They go on talking feverishly back and forth, joined and separated, talking words that come from different centers of being. Sonya has read to him from the New

Testament, read as a public confession the words of belief that Martha said to Jesus, words that she read as though they were her own and words that she read as though if Raskolnikov could say them as his own, his heart might open to love and he might believe. She said before him with religious feeling, "Yea, Lord: I believe that Thou art the Christ, the Son of God which should come into the world."

But Raskolnikov will not say such words as his own. She asks him after talking much what is to be done.

"What's to be done? Break what must be broken, once for all, that's all, and take the suffering on oneself. What, you don't understand? You'll understand later…Freedom and power, and above all, power. Over all trembling creation and the antheap!…That's the goal, remember that! That's my farewell message."

He is soon off away into the night after admitting to Sonya that he knows who murdered her friend Lizaveta and that if he comes back the next day, he will tell her who it is. But not for a moment does the idea enter her head that the murderer could be Raskolnikov. She is as extremely good in her thoughts as he is extremely bad in his.

He visits Sonya again at her room with the intention of confessing to her that he is the murderer of Lizaveta, her friend. But he is unable to confess the truth at once and instead tortures her with questions about who is worthy to live and who to die.

"'You better say straight out what you want!' Sonya cried in distress. 'You are leading up to something again…Can you have come simply to torture me?'"

But he is still unable to speak the truth. He is in a kind of delirium. He leads up to the confession but does not confess. Finally he makes her guess the truth. She is shocked but abandoning him is as far from her mind as the awful truth is now solidly established in her mind.

"'There is no one — no one in the whole world now so unhappy as you!' she cried in a frenzy…" She begins weeping.

"A feeling long unfamiliar to him flooded his heart and softened it at once. He did not struggle against it. Two tears started into his eyes and hung on his eyelashes.

'Then you won't leave me, Sonya?' he said, looking at her almost with hope.

'No, no, never, nowhere!' cried Sonya. 'I will follow you, I will follow you everywhere…'"

But for a few moments she can not believe he did it and asks him how it could have happened. He in turn has moments when he regrets letting her know the truth. She asks him to explain why he did it and he struggles to give her answers. She has touched his heart and brought tears to his eyes but he still is far from true redemption which is only possible if she can influence him to follow the feelings of his heart and discover the love that exists in his soul.

He goes into a long ramble to explain why he did it. "'And you don't suppose that I went into it headlong like a fool? I went into it like a wise man and that was just my destruction…I wanted to murder without casuistry, to murder for my own sake, for myself alone!…It wasn't to help my mother I did the murder…I wanted to find out something else; it was something else led me on. I wanted to find out then and quickly whether I was a louse like everybody else or a man. Whether I can step over barriers or not, whether I dare stoop to pick up or not, whether I am a trembling creature or whether I have the *right*…'

'To kill? Have the right to kill?' Sonya clasped her

hands.

'Ach, Sonia!' he cried irritably and seemed about to make some retort, but was contemptuously silent."

Sonia argues that he must go to the police and confess his guilt. But he has doubts about doing what she wants because at bottom he does not believe he is guilty. He has done the murder so intentionally, so rationally that guilt is impossible and redemption and divine forgiveness just as impossible. Sonya haunts him, following him in his movements around Petersburg whenever she can. Dostoevsky thus reverses the usual kind of haunting. Instead of the devil haunting a good soul, a good soul haunts a devil. She will not leave him ever. When Raskolnikov enters the police station finally to confess, he has second thoughts and leaves the building. Outside he sees Sonya standing not far from the entrance, "pale and horror-stricken. She looked wildly at him. He stood still before her. There was a look of poignant agony, of despair, in her face. She clasped her hands. His lips worked in an ugly, meaningless smile. He stood still a moment, grinned and went back to the police office."

At his trial he expresses no remorse or guilt for his crime. He is condemned to penal servitude in Siberia for eight years. Sonya follows him to Siberia and lives in a town near his prison. She lives only for him and does not bother him with thoughts about religion. Raskolnikov himself asks her after a year to lend him her copy of the New Testament. "It was the one from which she had read the raising of Lazarus to him." But he does not take it up and start reading it right away. Its influence may be in his future but only his imprisonment is now sure and Sonya haunting him and waiting for him nearby with nothing to sustain her except her *secret treasure*.

6

A main character in Dostoevsky's last novel, *The Brothers Karamazov*, Ivan Karamazov, says that if there is no God then we are free to do anything. The European existentialist philosophers took up this idea and held that all human acts must result from free choices since in a godless universe human being has no foundation. The French philosopher Jean-Paul Sartre went so far as to say that man is "condemned to be free". Dostoevsky held that freedom must be the supreme human value, but instead of denying the existence of God in order to act freely like some existentialists, he reasoned that finding God is possible if we reach a state of spiritual and intellectual freedom. The groundless freedom Dostoevsky felt in himself inspired him to create any kind of character ready to think or to do anything at all. Logical thought and free will result in human choices that create a world where human behavior is forced to follow a premeditated pattern dictated by reason. The more man accepts to live a life ruled by his reason and a knowledge arrived at using the same logic used by scientists, the less able he is to discover the world within him of God's divine grace which has nothing to do with reason and knowledge. God can control everything but he will not. He will not interfere with man's freedom to do and think whatever he wants. For Dostoevsky grace is a divine gift, a *secret treasure*, but total freedom is also a divine gift, perhaps a more important one. God gives humans his divine grace freely but he can not give it or he will not give it to people who live enslaved by a rationalized intentional way of living. Dostoevsky's rootless creations are enslaved by a power that does not originate in God.

Raskolnikov fascinates us because he appears free in a

way that is far beyond normal freedom. But his thoughts are transitory and negative. They rise up but are soon gone replaced by new thoughts and new ideas. His freedom grounded in his mind leads him nowhere, to an unreal inhuman state. He ultimately reveals that he is a fiction, a self freely created uselessly by a mind based on nothing. Sonya is free because the cruelty and the injustice of the world force her to be free. Insults, suffering, loathsomeness do not allow her mind to create for her some comforting fictitious but practical self based on nothingness. Everything has been taken from Sonya. The hatred and cruelty around her in the world have stripped her of normal human falsity and forced her to retreat into her soul. Because she must give up everything, she finds everything. The meek and the suffering inherit the world because the powerful of the world despise them and crush them. The world forces Sonya to flee into the nothingness in her soul where she discovers miraculously *a secret treasure.*

Some of Dostoevsky's other characters, like Sonya, give evidence of secret treasure within them but most of them are groundless, on their own, disconnected from the normal world and also from the world of God. He constructed characters from nothing and delighted in watching them try to assert their extreme individuality among regular, normal people. He created a comedy so divine that the more he created living beings from nothing, the more he became sure that God was helping him create them in order to show the world that nothing can ever be as vital as a divine presence in the human heart. For Dostoevsky life for humans must be free and without any foundation *because there is a God.*

In one of his early novels published in 1846, *The Double*, his hero Mr. Golyadkin, a minor government official, discovers the appearance of another Mr. Golyadkin, another being exactly like himself. At the beginning of the novel before his double appears, he consults a doctor because he feels mentally unbalanced. It is natural to think as his strange story develops that he loses his reason. In reality he never loses his reason and he becomes more and more unbalanced and delirious because he is horrified that he is losing not his reason but his self. His self appears to him in a form exactly like himself in every detail, as a living foreign himself exactly like himself. His double arrives on the scene and this other alien self that is also himself becomes more dominant in their relations with one another than himself. Reason is always able to guide us to some logical and practical end. We feel it is a necessary integral part of our normal behavior that helps us directly. But when our imagination runs wild for some unknown reason, when our emotions start going berserk and we appeal to our reason, we find that our reason is still present but is indifferent to our trouble and of no help. Mr. Golyadkin's reason tells him with indifference that he is the real Mr. Golyadkin and that the other Mr. Golyadkin is also the real Mr. Golyadkin. Reason does not abandon the poor man at all and merely remains a useless presence in his mind indifferent to the delirious state of his feelings. As the other false Mr. Golyadkin becomes more and more dominant and as the reason of the real Mr. Golyadkin is without any power to distinguish between the two and establish who is real and who is unreal, the feelings of the original Mr. Golyadkin go more and more berserk as he begins doubting that he is in fact real. He is forced to enter a mental hospital. His double walks behind the carriage bringing the original Mr. Golyadkin to his new home and as he arrives there, disappears. Dostoevsky's message is that Raskolnikov's self, Mr. Golyadkin's self, our selves may not be real. Our reason allows our imagination to create a self for ourselves and on our journey through life we must carefully keep presenting our invented self to others in a conventional package with few deviations. We feel comfortable with ourselves because other selves around us accept our invention of our self as real. Poor Mr. Golyadkin can not feel authentic facing his double's invention of himself because it is in fact himself and only he should have the right to invent himself! By way of contrast, Sonya's self is barely imaginable to herself. The self she constructed for herself naturally has been humiliated, crushed, destroyed. The world will no longer let her invent, it will only let her be. But normal being causes her suffering that is relieved only by the *secret treasure* she feels living in her heart. Unfortunately Raskolnikov and Mr. Golyadkin, who care nothing for the life of the heart, must rely only on themselves for strength and they discover that their inventions of themselves are not as reliable as they think.

The young Dostoevsky wrote *The Double* around the age of 25, two or three years before he received his second pair of eyes. As he stood before rifles pointed at him waiting for death, his reason at last allowed his imagination to abandon completely its duty to invent a self adapted to the selves of our world and let it go free to invent a self suitable to any world at all. A self for any world! But why not a self that did not fit in any world and that did not even need to make rational sense as a self? Bullets would fly at him in a few moments and when they arrived he would no longer have time or being or mind. The ground below his feet in seconds would no longer feel like ground. He would be timeless and groundless and his mind would no longer be able to pretend that rational forms of behavior were the only true basis of his true self.

8

Eighteen years after *The Double,* after four years of imprisonment at hard labor in Siberia, he wrote the short novel, *Notes From The Underground,* in which he takes up for treatment the subject of groundlessness. A man from the underground, from a corner of a room where he lives, like Raskolnikov, in self-isolation from the outside world, addresses us in a way that is extremely egotistical, proclaiming his complete freedom and his right to be irrational. He declares himself against not only all the normal customs of social life but also against all the natural laws of science and of mathematics. Unlike Raskolnikov, he uses his reason against reason, his logic against logic. "Merciful heavens!," he shouts at us, "But what do I care for the laws of nature and arithmetic when, for some reason, I dislike those laws and the fact that two times two makes four?" In other words, to hell with all laws! He lives in a corner of his room hidden away underground for forty years from the world outside. He has difficulty explaining to normal people the "strange enjoyment" that results from his lonely struggle. "But it is just in that cold, abominable half-despair, half-belief, in that conscious burying of oneself alive for grief in the underworld for forty years, in that acutely recognized and yet partly doubtful hopelessness of one's position, in that hell of unsatisfied desires turned inward, in that fever of oscillations, of resolutions determined for ever and repented of again a minute later — that the savor of that strange enjoyment of which I have spoken lies. It is so subtle, so difficult of analysis, that persons who are a little limited, or even simply persons of strong nerves, will not understand a single atom of it."

They will not understand that their selves hang floating in nothingness and that they can, like the man in the underground, strip themselves of every normal and decent and rational mental structure that creates for themselves and for others what they are. But the nothingness that the underground man opens up within himself when he kicks away both his normal invented self and the normal way people live does not fill up with some sort of blessed goodness. No, it fills with "half belief, half despair" and a "hell of unsatisfied desires turned inward". If you throw away the structures that make you yourself, you become defenseless. You become morbid and the world outside you that you despise and reject starts kicking you in the face because it no longer recognizes you as a normal person like all the normal persons around you who all resemble one another. Keep working at making your self yourself intentionally! It is what your mind tells you you must do!

The man from the underground shouts at us from Dostoevsky's pages daring, irrational, extremely egotistical thoughts. He hates the people around him and wants nothing to do with their normal, practical lives. "Advantage! What is advantage?" he asks us defiantly. "Can you possibly give an exact definition of the nature of human advantage? And what if *sometimes* a man's ultimate advantage not only may, but even must, in certain cases consist in his desiring something that is immediately harmful and not advantageous to himself?" There are some things, some experiences that escape all possible rational classification and when modern life will be so rationalized that all experience will have been rationally determined in advance, even then the man from the underground will not do automatically what he is supposed to do. He will not only not do what is to his advantage but he will seek what is not to his advantage. Against the whole world, against all the laws of society and science, against the power that tells us all *you must do this,* he, in his corner, he in his self-imposed prison, he will hold out against the power of two-plus-two-makes-four. He, when everyone else in the universe is doing only what reason tells them they must do, he will act willfully. He will will what he wants even if it is not to his advantage. Especially when it is not to his advantage because only then does he find a "strange enjoyment"!

"Well, can you expect a man who tries to find pleasure even in the feeling of his own humiliation to have an atom of respect for himself?" Humiliation humbles us. It makes us feel low and common. Someone just as low and common as ourselves suddenly inflicts an emotional wound on us that makes us feel painfully that we are even more low and common than everyone else. Our phony self is all at once sent flying out a window. Suddenly we no longer respect ourselves! What can be worse?

How can we live without respect for ourselves? Self-respect and self-esteem are the same thing and is there anything in the rationalized world we live in more necessary to be done with the power of love that exists in all of us than to love ourselves? The underground man not only has no self-respect but doesn't want any. Respect for himself will make him not only respect himself but respect others. To respect himself and to respect others means to respect a world ruled by reason. "You see, gentlemen," he tells us, "reason is an excellent thing. There is no doubt about it. But reason is only reason, and it can only satisfy the reasoning ability of man, whereas volition is a manifestation of the whole of life, I mean, of the whole of human life, including reason with all its concomitant head-scratchings…For my part, I quite naturally want to live in order to satisfy all my capacities for life and not my reasoning capacity alone, that is to say, only some twentieth part of my capacity for living. What does reason know? Reason only knows what it has succeeded in getting to know, whereas human nature acts as a whole, with everything that is in it, consciously, and unconsciously, and though it may commit all sorts of absurdities, it persists….man can deliberately and consciously desire something that is injurious, stupid, even outrageously stupid, just because he wants *to have the right* to desire for himself even what is very stupid and not to be bound by an obligation to desire only what is sensible." The underground man has no respect for his self unless it asserts itself on some occasions by acting willfully and he has come to enjoy willing what no one else dares to will. His humiliation has a "strange enjoyment" for him because when someone as common as himself puts him down, the pain to his wounded vanity also revives the life of his will that his reason tries to keep asleep.

He is now forty. Years before, when he was twenty-four, he was humiliated by an army officer. He goes by a small pub one night. He sees through a window some men having a fight with billiard cues and "one of them being thrown out a window". He feels "envious of the fellow who had been thrown out the window". Clearly it is not to his advantage to go into the pub and start a fight so that he can be himself thrown out a window. But that is what he wills, that is what he wants! He wants to teach his self the lesson that he does not respect it by acting willfully rather than rationally. But inside the pub he stands near the billiard tables and nothing happens. He does not start a fight. He does nothing to make someone throw him out a window. Without being aware of it, he is standing near a billiard table blocking the way. He is a "short, thin little fellow". An army officer over six feet, without any warning or explanation, picks up the underground man bodily and carries him to another place out of the way "as if I were a piece of furniture". He is "treated like a fly". His wounded vanity makes his heart burn with resentment and he can not rest until he dares to walk on purpose into the path of the officer one day on a crowded street bumping directly against him. He gets the worst of the bumping but he is nonetheless strangely satisfied. He gets enjoyment by daring to act willfully and unreasonably in a way that upsets normal behavior.

Such strokes of the will against the world are impossible as long as the underground man hides alone in his corner brooding. He too, like Raskolnikov, gets up, goes out, and tests whether or not his thoughts and what he wills count for anything in a world where humans think very little and very rarely accomplish what they really and truly will. In fact, he is in no hurry to rush out and involve himself in the real world. Instead, he passes three months dreaming, dreaming of what he calls "salvation through the good and the beautiful". "But how much love, good Lord, how much love I used to experience in those dreams of mine." "...fantastic though that sort of love was and though in reality it had no relation whatsoever to anything human, there was so much of it, so much of this love, that one did not feel the need of applying it in practice afterwards…" However, after three months of dreaming, he feels "an irresistible urge to plunge into social life". That the man from the underground will meet real love in the real world seems impossible but for Dostoevsky that is the only place real love can exist. The love that the underground man has been experiencing in his dreaming is an unreal result of poetic fantasy and for Dostoevsky there is no such thing as "salvation through the good and the beautiful". However, he never rules out anything happening to anyone in the real world, even love for a "short, thin little fellow" like his underground man.

He decides to contact former schoolfellows whom he has not seen for years. He despises them all, Simonov, whom he suspects loathes him, Ferfichkin, "a little fellow with the face of a monkey" who was one of his worst enemies from their earliest days at school, Trudolyubov, an army officer, " a great admirer of every kind of success and only capable of discussing promotions". He visits Simonov and finds the three of them discussing a dinner party for a fourth, Zverkov. They make plans for the dinner party in his presence without inviting him. He is forced to invite himself and the three are forced to accept him unwillingly. The underground man describes the four of them hatefully and scorns them for their lack of intelligence and for their lack of respect for himself. But he is by no means a model of goodness and polite behavior! He uses the dinner party as a scene to display his willfulness with continuous critical words and strange acts that are clearly not to his advantage or anyone's advantage. He insults them and even challenges one to a duel. The four end up not speaking to him at all. All of them eat and drink a great deal. After dinner the four leave the table and sit at a sofa drinking and talking and ignoring the underground man. He decides to pace up and down the room opposite the sofa. "*They* paid no attention to me. I had the patience to pace the room… right in front of them from eight till eleven o'clock, always in the same place, from the table to the stove, and back again." Acting willfully in the real world requires a will willing to experience anything no matter how painful. In comparison, rational behavior is as gracious as it is boring.

The four decide to leave the restaurant for an adventurous evening of vice. They do not invite the underground man who hesitates to follow them. When he finally decides to follow them and arrives at their destination, the four have gone. He falls asleep and wakes up seeing "two wide-open eyes observing me intently and curiously. The look in those eyes was coldly indifferent and sullen, as though it were utterly detached, and it made me feel terribly depressed." "I suddenly saw clearly how absurd and hideous like a spider was the idea of vice which, without love, grossly and shamelessly begins where true love finds its consummation." He remembers that for two hours he "had never said a word to this creature, and had not even thought it necessary to do so".

Now however he does talk to her. He asks her name. "'Lisa', she replied, almost in a whisper, but somehow without attempting to be agreeable, and turned her eyes away." He finds it "hideous" to talk to her and he goes on asking details about her life "almost angry with her". She gives him information about her background speaking "more and more abruptly". He tells her of a burial he observed of a girl her own age who had been living in a similar set of circumstances. This makes her curious but she asks him questions about the burial "speaking even more abruptly and harshly than before". Something however eggs him on to carry on the conversation. Will he speak willfully with her? Will he speak egotistically and hostily to her as he has been speaking to his school fellows a few hours before at the dinner party? Will he test his highly individualistic antisocial amoral ideas on her to perhaps influence her to live as he does delighting in groundlessness and irrationality? What kind of talk will come from the underground man now that he has left his hiding place and must talk to a real woman in a real world? If he does not continue his wild and crazy antisocial talk, will he not prove to us that he has been nothing but all talk? But on the other hand, he can not be humiliated by her in the present situation where he is dominant and she is a young woman with a lowly status. Since he can not find a "strange enjoyment" from some humiliation caused him by a prostitute, he tries to influence her to rise above her lowly state.

In the presence of the young woman, the underground man turns into a run of the mill idealistic moralist! He turns himself into a new man, a regular honest middle-class man, as he begins describing for her the joys possible if she changes and lives a pure and honest life! "Come, get back your senses while there's still time. You're still young, you're good-looking, you might fall in love, be married, be happy…" He is disgusted with the way he is talking. He regrets that he is "no longer reasoning coldly" and that he himself was feeling what he was saying and "warmed to the subject". But he goes on and on painting for her verbal images in long moralizing speeches about the joys of a normal life with love, marriage and the love of children. He tells us that his "moralizing" is "ridiculous" and that she probably doesn't understand any of it but he goes on anyway. "Though you are now young, attractive, pretty, sensitive, warm-hearted, I — well, you know, the moment I woke up a few moments ago, I couldn't help feeling disgusted at being with you here!…But if you were anywhere else, if you lived as all good, decent people live, I should not only have taken a fancy to you, but fallen head over heels in love with you."

"I knew I was speaking in a stiff, affected, even bookish manner, but as a matter of fact I could not speak except 'as though I was reading from a book'. But that did not worry me, for I knew, I had a feeling that I would be understood, that this very bookishness would assist rather than hinder matters." Eventually he sees that he has made an impression on her and it frightens him because her body "was writhing as though in convulsions". She sobs and "broke out into loud moans and cries". He can not go on with his "bookish" talk because he sees fearfully that it is having a real effect on a real human being. He is about to tell her that he is sorry, that he should not have talked to her so long in such a positive moralistic idealistic fashion but he stops realizing that he has had a real effect on her and that now it would be wrong to try to undo what he has done. He gives her his address and tells her to come and see him. She will not let him go until she relates a story about how she once was loved by a young man before she sank to her present condition. Her story proves that now because of the underground man's positive sermon she has hope for a changed future. He is sorry for what he has done and is happy to leave.

Away from Lisa, he is "overcome with embarrassment" for what he has said to her. How could he have talked for so long so sentimentally with romantic nonsense about goodness and love and hope? He gave her his address and now is worried that she will come to visit him. Even as days pass and she still does not come, he remains worried. "If not today, then tomorrow, but come she will! She'll seek me out! For such is the damned romanticism of all those *pure hearts*!…How could she fail to understand? Why, anyone would have seen through it!"

When Lisa visits him and they sit together with tea, he has a nervous attack and begins sobbing. "She was frightened. 'What's the matter? What's the matter?' she kept asking, standing helplessly over me." He resents her presence and there are long silences between them. Finally she speaks. "'I–I want to get away from that place for good,' she began in an effort to do something to break the silence, but, poor thing, that was just what she should not have spoken about at such a stupid moment and especially to a man who was as stupid as I." Another five minutes of silence passes between them. He asks her suddenly what she has come for and she does not answer. "I'll tell you, my dear girl, what you have come for. You've come because I made *pathetic speeches* to you the other night. So you were softened and now you want more of these pathetic speeches. Well, I may as well tell you at once I was laughing at you then. And I'm laughing at you now….I had been insulted before, at dinner, by the fellows who came before me that night….So to avenge my wounded pride on someone, to get my own back, I vented my spite on you and I laughed at you. I had been humiliated, so I wanted to humiliate someone…I wanted power. Power was what I wanted then. I wanted sport. I wanted to see you cry. I wanted to humiliate you. To make you hysterical….And do you realize that now that I've told you all this I shall hate you for having been here and listened to me?"

He crushes her and humiliates her but his actions strip

her of any power to defend herself and because she is now without anything even approaching a reasonable well-ordered respect for herself, because he has forced her to slip into the irrational side of her nature and come directly in contact with her soul, she loves! The eyes of her soul let her see that behind all his negative talk against her and against himself, is *a man who is suffering.* She loves! She holds out her hands to him. She rushes at him, throws her arms around him, and bursts into tears. He begins sobbing "as I had never in my life sobbed before". He falls on the sofa and sobs for a quarter of an hour. She clings to him and puts her arms around him and seems "to remain frozen in that embrace".

So the underground man has been all talk! His reason and his heart and his soul live in him harmoniously with one another as they do in us and just like we he too can love and love will certainly change him and teach him self-respect! Two lost unhappy souls are now saved! The "bookish" idealistic world is the true world! The world of the "good and the beautiful" is real! Groundlessness and irrationality and willfulness have no place in the world of goodness and love! The real world has finally revealed itself to Lisa and the man from the underground!

He lies on the sofa and is ashamed to look at her. He is ashamed! It occurs to him "that our parts were now completely changed, that she was the heroine now, while I was exactly the same crushed and humiliated creature as she had appeared to me that night — four days before". He envies her! "I cannot live without feeling that I have someone completely in my power, that I am free to tyrannize over some human being." In his heart blazes up a feeling of domination and possession. "I clasped her hands violently. How I hated her and how I was drawn to her at that moment!…At first she looked bewildered and even frightened, but only for one moment. She embraced me warmly and rapturously."

A quarter hour later Lisa is sitting on the floor leaning her head against the edge of the bed crying. The underground man is impatient with her and wants her to leave. "This time she knew everything. I had insulted her finally…She guessed that my outburst of passion was nothing but revenge, a fresh insult for her, and that to my earlier, almost aimless, hatred, there was now added a *personal, jealous* hatred of her….However, I can't be certain that she did understand it all so clearly; what she certainly did understand was that I was a loathsome man and that, above all, I was incapable of loving her."

Just as Raskolnikov cannot simply love Sonya, the man from the underground cannot seize the love that Lisa offers him and love her! He too is gone, removed like Raskolnikov from the human, because he is incapable of ruling himself as normal people do with his reason. Even when the body of a young attractive woman embraces him weeping full of love, he must act willfully. He insults her with his lust when he should have respected her and himself by giving way not to lust but to love. But even as Lisa cries leaning her head on the edge of the bed, all is not lost. Moments of lust do not kill love if it is real and Lisa despite his hatred and jealousy does love him. In spite of his need to be willful, how can he resist a miracle when it falls on him from out of nowhere? It is perhaps only the second act in the drama of Lisa and the underground man and other acts can still follow and can produce a happy ending.

She comes from the bed and looks at him hard. He smiles at her maliciously. She says goodbye and goes to the door but before she can reach it, he runs up to her and puts money in her hand. Then he rushes away from the door. She leaves. He says that he put what he put in her hand "not because my heart, but because my wicked brain prompted me to do it". But soon, overwhelmed with shame, he rushes out the door after her. He calls to her down the staircase but receives no answer. When he returns to his rooms, he discovers on the table near the door the five-rouble note which minutes before he had pressed into her hand.

He acts willfully with the world and experiences a strange enjoyment but he acts rationally with a woman who loves him and learns that his heart is empty. But he is a hero nonetheless the underground man. The world demands that he act moderately and rationally and women demand that he love. He can do neither and he refuses to live falsely. Groundlessness is painful but it is at least free. The underground man lives where he must live, underground where the struggles to reach the deep things of the soul live and where the idealistic and "bookish" lights from the world of the "good and the beautiful" never shine.

9

Dostoevsky confessed that his belief came from "the fire of doubt". His belief in God went hand in hand with doubt but his belief in Russia and his belief that without the Russian Orthodox church there could be no Russia were not subject to doubt. How could Sonya with little education and experience have found the *secret treasure* within her if there were no church that transmitted from generation to generation religious practices and kept the possibility of goodness and genuine religious experience alive? The religious experience offered by church rituals and the unity of Russia politically under the Tzar seemed essential to Dostoevsky even if the political system was far from perfect and even though the rituals of the church produced only lukewarm experience. But the goodness that resulted from the public presence of the church did not lead him to the mystery of creation. His "second pair of eyes" drove him to look for truth against nature and in what was behind and hidden from normal eyes.

However in his novel, *The Idiot*, Dostoevsky tests for us the fate of a man who is genuinely and totally good. His hero, Prince Myshkin, is so good that his extreme goodness is as much a flaw in his character as was extreme rationality in the case of Raskolnikov or extreme willfulness in the case of the Underground Man. The Prince returns to Russia after a long absence in Switzerland and becomes directly involved with several normal people in Saint Petersburg society who are relating to one another trying to resolve regular problems of life. The Prince gets caught personally in their emotional conflicts. He interacts with them with such complete honesty and total goodness that he ends by not helping them but harming them. He is so good he can not fit in regular society. His Christian goodness erodes the power of his human will and isolates him tragically from normal people.

The goodness of the prince was a part of Dostoevsky's nature but only a part. The other part, the part that was irrational and willful and a fervent enemy of two-plus-two-makes-four is expressed in the novel by a young man named Hippolyte. He is near death because in the last stages of tuberculosis. Facing death, he wants nothing to do with any talk of accepting any law of nature or any spiritual compensation that might give him in his final living moments peace and the comforts of religion by accepting submissively his fate. Lying on his deathbed, he describes to prince Myshkin the sufferings of Christ as he hung on the cross. He talks to the prince about how Christ looked in his death agony in a painting they both have observed closely. Christ's face is disfigured by the blows he received and is bloodied. His wide open eyes have a deathly look. Hippolyte asks how his mother and his disciples at the foot of his cross could possibly believe he could resurrect himself from the dead. The laws of nature are terrible. Christ on the cross cried out in agony, "My God, my God, why have thou forsaken me?" Nature seems to Hippolyte like an enormous beast, pitiless and silent, or like a terrible machine designed to destroy humans and even destroy Christ who was an infinitely good and admirable being full of holiness. Hippolyte despises the laws of nature and refuses to accept them with humility. He agrees with the Underground Man who said, "The laws of nature have continually all my life offended me more than anything else". "What is the tribunal that judges here?" asks Hippolyte. "Why is it necessary that I not only be condemned but that I support my condemnation without protesting?...What good is humility?...Why am I supposed to sing the praises of forces that are devouring me?" Prince Myshkin offers him resignation and goodness but he cannot affect Hippolyte positively. Dostoevsky again creates in his works good characters like Prince Myshkin, like the young monk Alyosha in *The Brothers Karamazov,* but the side of him that created Hippolyte was the source of most of his characters. He had a double nature that tormented him with conflicts that he could not resolve but he bravely explored the side of himself that was not good because that was where he believed the key to the mystery of creation lived and where he could somehow even experience the mystery.

10

A great writer, faced with the exterior disunity of his country, struggles to give his readers the sense that a unity nonetheless can exist. He proves in his artistic works that national unity is a real possibility by somehow integrating dramatically many individuals with separate and contrary individual characters. Shakespeare put all of England in his works even though the unity is there piecemeal, bit by bit, individual by individual, one passion here, one there. Together with his attempt to express England universally, he did however define England concretely by incorporating in his works one hero who expressed individually most of the various feelings and dramatic conflicts possible among the English. Hamlet's sufferings and struggles with himself and with others to find and establish his true identity make us feel also England's sufferings struggling to become England. In the final act after Hamlet has passed through many conflicts and declares finally and maturely, "readiness is all", we feel along with him what England must be to be England, solid, secure, rational, ready to bravely face anything. Dante unified Italy by taking it poetically through its hells, its purgatories and its heavenly ascents. James Joyce put all of Ireland's trials and struggles with itself into the ups and downs of its people during one day in Dublin and he makes us feel that the Irish soul must forever wander in foreign territories like Ulysses. Tolstoy's great novels give us universally the feelings of Russians at peace and at war with themselves. Dostoevsky at the time when he was about to create his greatest work, his novel *The Possessed*, had already produced works with portraits of Russians of all types. But he had mainly concentrated on creating extraordinary individuals at the center of great works, Raskolnikov, Golyadkin, the Underground Man, Prince Myshkin. In *The Possessed* he centers the novel not on one individual hero but on three. The search among three young men for communication and love between themselves and their tragic failure to achieve this objective is the main theme of the work. Around Dostoevsky as he wrote *The Possessed* he saw the signs of Russian society beginning to come apart. Socialist revolutionaries and other revolutionaries with various new modern ideologies were threatening traditional political, economic and religious values. A tragedy was taking place before his regular eyes that threatened to radically change Russia. But his "second pair of eyes" also examined the troubles of Russia. They showed him that behind the revolutionary stirrings and the social upheaval Russians were expressing hidden in their hearts a need for brotherly love. He decided to relate with his regular pair of eyes the regular goings on in a provincial society while at the same time his "second pair of eyes" created below and hidden in the same society a group of revolutionaries plotting secretly to destroy regular Russian society and create a new Russia. Dostoevsky ridicules them and portrays them as possessed by foolish ideas based on nothingness. But he nonetheless agreed in his heart with their desire for the future brotherly unity of Russia. He disagreed that socialism could ever produce it. His "second pair of eyes" saw that a Christ-like brotherly love was possible. His regular pair of eyes saw clearly that such a love was impossible but he decided anyway to try to express it in his three heroes, Stavrogin, Shatov and Kirillov He put most of the conflicts of the Russia of his time into this his greatest work. It is a gigantic display of every type of disunity possible among humans enslaved by false ideas about both their true selves and about the true needs of Russia. No Christ-like love for one another takes place in the souls of his three heroes. Disunity rules universally just as though everyone is possessed by a devil.

Two extraordinary creations in *The Possessed* are unlike anything ever produced in any literature. First, Dostoevsky creates a non-marriage marriage between a man and a woman that lasts for twenty-two years but deteriorates as the non-wife wife gradually loses respect for her non-husband husband. Second, the woman in the false non-marriage marriage gives birth to a son whose real father, legally married to her, never appears in the novel. Her son, Nicholas Stavrogin, is presented to us as a non-Christ Christ. The false non-marriage marriage is never consummated sexually and the male's masculinity is drastically diminished by the female who dominates him at the beginning of their sentimental friendship and grows steadily more dominant. The son she has produced from her womb by an absent father is presented to us as a false Christ who ends his life like Christ willing his own death. Even more extraordinary, the false Christ has conversations about deep subjects with Shatov and Kirillov that influence them profoundly and change forever the direction of their lives even though he, the false Christ, does not believe the ideas his own words express. The false Christ gathers to himself by joining a revolutionary socialist group apostles who become his devoted disciples even though at bottom he is not interested in their revolutionary ideas at all. But the height of the extraordinary comes as the result of a long conversation between Stavrogin, the false Christ, and his disciple

Shatov when a non-christian converts another non-christian by sending him on a path towards Christian belief even though he, the false Christ, Stavrogin, the non-christian who causes the conversion, is himself an atheist.

Dostoevsky's theme in *The Possessed* is the futile searching of men and women for the brotherly unification promised by the appearance on earth of divinity in Christ. Christ said, "Whenever two men are together in my name, I am among them." This means that two men can be joined in a Christ-like love, that they can break through barriers that separate them and reach into each other's soul. They can become one in the Body of Christ through the spiritual power of the Holy Spirit instituted on earth as the result of Christ's sacrifice on the cross. Dostoevsky has three heroes in *The Possessed* very close to one another personally but tragically unable to unite spiritually. Kirillov and Shatov have a strong spiritual and psychological dependence on the third hero, Stavrogin. He has influenced their inner being deeply by both his presence among them and his words and thoughts but he is in his being strangely inhuman and aloof from all regular feelings and is incapable of matching their feelings for him. If the three could become one spirit, each could perhaps find a new freedom and a new self but they cannot make a leap of faith from their own being into the heart of another being and each remains alone and spiritually destitute. Dostoevsky also takes up the same theme of the search for the spiritual communication of three men, of three brothers, in his last novel, *The Brothers Karamazov. The Possessed* on the surface is about the failed search for brotherly unity among a group of socialist revolutionaries. But Dostoevsky knew and all Christians know that the only real brotherhood is a brotherhood that derives from fearless believing souls full of love open to all souls and yearning to implant love from one soul in another soul as did Christ. He walked among men and implanted his divine love in their souls. The brotherly unity of the souls of all the Russians was what Dostoevsky wanted with all his soul but even though he knew it was impossible to create this unity either in Russia or in his novel, he tried to create it anyway. The result is the story of Christ's life and death repeated and redesigned with a false Christ and false apostles that results in unholy deaths that do nothing to strengthen Russian Christianity and instead reveal the ghastly disunity of Russia in a work that is nonetheless the highest achievement of Russian literature.

11

Dostoevsky begins *The Possessed* with a long description of Stepan Trafimovich Verhovensky's life as a man who fails as a husband, a writer, a revolutionary, and a college lecturer. It is an amusing description of someone of Dostoevsky's generation that came of age in the 1840s. However at the same time it is a description of a man, based on the narrator's intimate knowledge of his being, that makes us see clearly by concrete details tracing the key points of his biography that he has no authentic being of his own. Every fact we receive about his life can only make us conclude that his very life itself is a fake. His generation, the generation young in the 1840s, had little success with its revolutionary views for a new Russia and has now been surpassed by a new generation with new revolutionaries. Stepan Trofimovich is well educated, has elegant manners, and speaks French like a Parisian. He has gained some minor fame as a leading exponent of the new ideas among revolutionaries of the 1840s but that fame has faded. Varvara Petrovna Stavrogin, his friend and benefactor, lives completely removed from her legal husband, General Stavrogin. He does not appear in any scene in the novel and it is as though he does not exist. Varvara Petrovna has been inspired as a young woman by poetic raptures after contact with writers expressing the idealistic and romantic ideas of the 1840s. She develops a friendship with Stepan Trafimovitch based mainly on her belief that he is a leading spirit of the times. She supports Stepan Trafimovitch financially for twenty-two years. He lives first in her house and later in a separate small house she provides him next to her house. As the novel begins in the 1850s Stepan Trofimovich is forgotten in revolutionary circles. He lives off his friend Varvara Petrovna on her estate in a province in a rural area. Out in the country away from big cities, Stepan Trafimovich enjoys imagining himself as a revolutionary in hiding from authorities. This is completely false. He is not suspected of revolutionary activity by authorities. The fact that he is playing the role of someone in exile out in a province and using his fictitious persecution as justification for his intellectual inactivity simply adds more weight to the general inauthenticity and falsity of his identity. His complete financial dependency on his rich friend Varvara Petrovna also makes his own sense of worth fragile. Early in their union which lasts so many years, he and Varvara Petrovna spend a winter in Saint Petersburg to try to understand the new types of revolutionaries and to perhaps become involved themselves at the forefront of the new ideas. The other reason for their trip is that Varvara Petrovna's son, Nicholas Stavrogin, is in a school in Petersburg. They attend literary evenings but are unable to understand the daring ideas of the new people. When Stepan Trafimovich gives a public lecture, he is laughed at. They escape from the countless minor devils in Petersburg enslaved by the new revolutionary socialist principles and return to their province where there are also many of the same kind of devils comfortably hidden behind the normalcy of their provincial society.

Varvara Petrovna Stavrogin, except in the period when she gave birth to her son Nicholas Stavrogin, lives a virginal and pure life, almost a holy life. She lives apart from her legal husband. When he dies she observes in her friend Stepan Trofimovich from certain nuances in their conversations that he is seriously thinking of a real marriage with his extremely rich friend. She rebuffs him rudely. Their relationship is not an ordinary one and we are forced by its extraordinary quality to suspect that it has been constructed by Dostoevsky with the parents of Christ in mind. In Varvara Petrovna we can make out a false Mary, a mother of a false Christ who like the holy Mary of Scripture is a mother who gives birth to a son without an actual father. If Varvara Petrovna is a false Mary then Stepan Trafimovich fits nicely as a false Joseph, the husband of the holy Mary of the New Testament who is nonetheless not the father of Christ. Stepan Trofimovich does tutor young Nicholas Stavrogin throughout his childhood and thus acts as a substitute father of a false Christ as did Joseph the substitute father of the real Christ.

Stavrogin, the son of Varvara Petrovna by a father who never appears, must be understood as a false Christ. This Christ in reverse will draw to himself converts by the strength like Christ of his powerful personhood. Three of the main socialist revolutionaries, Pyotr Stepanovitch Verhovensky, Kirillov and Shatov look up to him with a kind of diabolical devotion even though his person has nothing at its bottom except nothingness. He expresses to the three at various times in various circumstances ideas on various subjects including religious ideas about the real Christ that influence his disciples Kirillov and Shatov deeply even though he himself believes them not at all. This structure of the plot containing a Christ in reverse and elements of the Christian religion in reverse is not hidden by Dostoevsky. The title in Russian is one word, *Besie,* the word for devils. Since all the characters are devilish beings deluded by the belief that they are normal, it makes artistic sense to have at the center a super devil who alone remains true to himself because he can never escape the nothingness in his soul that continually screams at him that he is nothing. The other characters in the novel are to various degrees possessed by a devil who provides them with the illusion that they are all a something. Our false Christ, Stavrogin, in a meeting one night with his closest disciple, Shatov, actually produces at the end of their long powerful emotional and spiritual dialogue a profound moment of love and conversion in the soul of Shatov that should not happen. It is in fact not a real *Christian* conversion at all and yet is a powerful transformation of a soul before our eyes caused by a false Christ that takes us in our feelings beyond time. Since Dostoevsky actually creates this false conversion in the soul of Shatov caused by his love for a false Christ, a false conversion that is psychologically powerful, we cannot escape noticing that this is more evidence of the story of a false Christ that he is structuring. The conversion of Shatov is a failed Christian conversion, an "almost" Christian conversion, just as Raskolnikov was almost converted by Sonya or as the Underground Man almost found love with Lisa. But the "almost" conversion of Shatov who is the soul of Russia in person does take us in our feelings because of

Dostoevsky's wild and free inspiration "almost" to the real brotherly spiritual union possible "almost" between all Russian souls. The work is a bible of Russian atheism and nihilism. The focus on the surface is on the plotting of sincere socialists for brotherly union in a socialist state. Dostoevsky ridicules their ideals but his ideal is "almost" the same as theirs. He also wants brotherly union and tries to achieve it in relationships between his three heroes. He "almost" achieves it in a scene late at night between Shatov and Stavrogin, a scene that we will describe in detail later. The work is "almost" about the unity of Russia but instead is about its disunity. Shatov "almost" converts to Christianity but instead is murdered by the group of revolutionaries led by the son of Stepan Trofimovich Verhovensky. What name does Dostoevsky choose for this leader of the group of false apostles who are devoted "almost" religiously to a false Christ? Pyotor Stepanovitch Verhovensky. Pyotor is the Russian for "Peter". *Stavros* in Greek means "cross" and in its verbal form it can mean "to crucify". Stavrogin's terrible cross he must bear is a being that cannot relate genuinely human to human to any human and his lonely and empty being is as far removed from the blessed world of God as the devil himself.

12

The Tzar held Russian society together and when he freed the serfs in 1861 Dostoevsky described his act as "blessed'. He creates in *The Possessed* not only a Christ in reverse, a false Christ, but also a Tzar in reverse. A young aristocrat, whose mother Varvara Petrovna is the most wealthy landowner of his province, is the main young aristocratic figure of the area's society. He has the potential to hold the provincial society together morally by his examples of nobility and goodness. Everyone looks to him for guidance, but then, even though his character superficially appears to be that of a normal aristocrat, he reveals by strange abnormal acts in public observed publically that his character is in reality groundless and that he is capable of doing anything willfully like the man from the underground. Young Stavrogin's inner character contains little more than a despicable moral nothingness producing an abnormal and insane detachment from the normal behavior of those around him. This false Christ is capable like the real Christ of being only an imitation of a man rather than a real human man. He does despicable things like Raskolnikov and the man from the underground, and like the Underground Man he is unable to love a young woman who offers herself to him. He is truly a Christ and a Tzar in reverse, a leader who does not wish to lead anyone and whose devilish groundlessness is incapable of leading himself to anything except suicide.

The Possessed, a bible of nineteenth-century Russian nihilism and atheism, is written to show that atheism and nothingness are the same thing. One of the three heroes, Shatov, reaches bravely into his own groundlessness and almost makes a leap of faith to become a believing Christian. But all the characters are fatally groundless to one degree or another. Dostoevsky was fascinated by the idea that freedom from belief in God automatically leads to slavery although atheists think denying God is the necessary first step towards freedom. Even though freedom is dangerous because it can lead to godlessness and nihilism, freedom became nonetheless Dostoevsky's ultimate *religious* value. For him there could be no true religious belief that was not reached freely by someone who dared to admit his nothingness and called to God from the depths of his soul for divine help. Being religious meant being in touch with a *secret treasure* within but since the world without was irreligious and hostile to all secret inner treasures, freedom became the only weapon available to him to fight against the way people lived in a godless world. *The Possessed* reveals Dostoevsky's new religion of freedom by proving that nihilistic atheism leads only to slavery. Man's freedom can become a true and real freedom only by enslaving himself to God and to God's creation which is full of grace. A person's self creation without divine grace is an illusion and the world's creations are based on nothingness.

In *The Possessed,* Pyotor Stepanovich Verhovensky, the estranged son of Stepan Trofimovich Verhovensky, leads a group of local revolutionary conspirators. He holds them together by making them believe that they are just one local group of a vast revolutionary organization over all of Russia and that he is in direct contact with the leaders of the central committee. Outwardly they are socialist revolutionaries but in Dostoevsky's partially hidden plan to mirror in the regular story the story of Christ, they are Christian apostles in reverse. It is not God who creates the revolutionaries, the false apostles, Pyotor Stepanovich creates them. He guides himself, like Raskolnikov, only with his reason and is indifferent to everything that is living, creative, enthusiastic, romantic, passionate. His reason has manipulated his mind and settled him in a comfortable bourgeois sort of atheism. He uses logic as a devilish weapon to manipulate everyone in his secret band of revolutionaries except Stavrogin. He worships Stavrogin satanically with a diabolical love. He dreams in fact of making him a new Tzar, an usurper of the Tzar's political power through revolution. Nothingness is as comfortable in Pyotor Stepanovich as atheism and reason and he has no interest at all in creating a revolutionary group to produce good. Stavrogin is an atheist by indifference. He is indifferent to everything, religion, revolution, social status, love, life. He is bored by everyone and everything and is interested in the revolutionary group only as a relief from his boredom. He does however, like the man from the underground, enjoy acting willfully and basely because only base behavior provides him intense sensations. Shatov has been a socialist revolutionary like the other members of the group but he has had a change of heart. He now believes in the presence of a divine soul mysteriously alive in the Russian people. His love of Russia and its people, his Slavophilism, and his fervent conviction that Russia is in danger of being contaminated by western ideas and beliefs has driven him to worship passionately the national soul of Russia. He is very close to conversion to Christianity and believes already in a messianic destiny for Russia. Shatov fights with his whole soul against Western European cultural influences but he never surrenders his soul to God and discovers real freedom. He believes an Apocalypse is coming that will purify Russia from all contamination but he is murdered by Pyotor Stepanovich's group before he has a chance to perhaps achieve genuine Christian belief. Kirillov is the most extraordinary atheist in Pyotor Stepanovich's group of revolutionaries. He is a Christ-like atheist. He has decided to commit suicide. He will kill himself not out of despair but as the logical result of his philosophical thoughts. "If God doesn't exist," says Kirillov, "I am God." He believes men invented God only in order to be able to live without fear of death and without killing themselves. If Kirillov kills himself indifferently, he will prove to humanity that total freedom is possible.

The two things that torture man are the fear of death and the fear of what may lie beyond death. Kirillov wants to eliminate these fears by committing suicide voluntarily which will prove to humanity that it can overcome by its own free will its terrible fears and every man can become God.

These four groundless and atheistic young men as well as other atheistic revolutionaries, other false Christian apostles, reveal that they possess no inner dimension that gives a special unique nuance to their being. They have none of them any true self. Dostoevsky in his novel *The Brothers Karamazov* writes of Alyosha Karamazov, a devout Christian who plans to become a monk in a local monastery, that he wishes "to escape the lot of those who have lived their whole life without finding their true selves in themselves." Our true self is not automatically the same as our self. The true self or nothingness are the opposite poles behind all of Dostoevsky's creations. He created atheistic characters because atheism is a denial not only of God but also of the existence of one's true self. The atheist however will not admit that the denial of God is also a denial of his true self. On the contrary, it is perfectly clear to the atheist that to deny God is to assert the self. And it is! Except that the self that the atheist asserts so forcefully is not the true self! A self that acts in a purely rational and objective manner can not be a true self, a real person. It seems ironic that Mr. Golyadkin emerges more and more as an authentic person when his double appears and makes him begin doubting his own existence. He begins doubting that his self is his true self when he is forced to think it may be foreign to him by appearing before him in a foreign being. Tragedy and suffering and fear sometimes force people to give up reliance on their false selves and force them to seek their true self. Raskolnikov and the man from the underground struggle passionately to assert themselves, in Raskolnikov's case, by a reliance only on reason, in the Underground Man's case, by using his reason to aid him to act willfully. But neither of them dare to cut the cord that binds them to a false self that might allow them some creative spiritual vision of who they are really. Sonya emerges as a real person because she no longer has power to assert a false self that others have crushed. Lisa reveals she is a real person by leaving behind on the Underground Man's table the five roubles that he has pressed into her hand as she is leaving. We all have a quality that mysteriously renders us distinct from everyone else but we accept this quality as natural although it is mysterious. We know rationally that we are each of us distinct but reason alone can never open the path to our true self. Only surrendering ourselves unconditionally to God as did Abraham in the Bible unites us both to God and to our true self. A divine and unique personhood can shine forth like an aura within anyone who has the courage to accept in his soul the nothingness at the heart of being and to will to do no longer what he wants to do but what God wants him to do. God is the author of everything and his most awesome and most fundamental creation is the divine and unique spiritual personhood hidden in us which is revealed by divine grace. Union with God is also union with the true self and at the same time a revelation in the soul of a divine freedom. The atheists in *The Possessed* have lost touch with God and grace and their characters can be expressed fairly easily by Dostoevsky as fictions because they are of their own condition fictional characters. Fictional beings can easily take a perfect form. Personhood is a mysterious gift from God that is perfect inwardly but outwardly is never objectively perfect.

All the main characters of *The Possessed* are false selves out of touch with their own authentic personhood. None of them know who they are although they all use reason to establish before others some sort of objective self. None of them are real persons. Pyotor Stepanovich, the leader of the revolutionary group, is the most rational nihilist. His behavior is so solidly grounded in his reason that he suggests by his depersonalized actions that personhood is an illusion. His father, Stepan Trofimovich, by contrast, begins revealing himself more and more as a real person as his vain and false self is ridiculed both by his own son and Varvara Petrovna, his false wife, and shown to be ineffectual, ridiculous and ignoble. The profound message that Dostoevsky sends us in *The Possessed* is that we are all devils, that we are possessed by something, that something has created all of us and that as long as we continue to submit to this something we make ourselves nothing. Freedom alone can send us on the true path to life but instead we lock ourselves in a prison and give our reason the key.

Stepan Trofimovich's's enemy, the antagonist who drives him to a state of total economic dependence and to a condition of emotional frustration and humiliation, is his lifelong friend, Varvara Petrovna. Stepan Trofimovich's male emotions are frustrated and humiliated continually by his female friend to a state of pitiful sentimental ineffectuality. However he remains loyal to his friend, his antagonist. She remains loyal to him until in the end after twenty-two years she "divorces" him, telling him frankly that she will never again have anything to do with him, but in the scene of their breakup she also settles a lifelong pension on him. He always gives way to her against his will and sinks lower and lower in his own estimation of himself. She creates him. She designs his clothing. She supports him during most of his adult life with her money. He endures painfully the signs and acts on her part that reveal that his lifelong friend with whom he has shared the purest and most noble sentiments of his heart respects him less and less. In the end Stepan Trofimovich is forced by circumstances to search for his true self against his will. If Stavrogin, Varvara Petrovna's son is a debased version of the Tzar, Stepan Trofimovich might be likened to a debased version of the great Russian writer Leo Tolstoy. Tolstoy sought the true self too. He suspected all his life that he was lacking some quality, some mysterious element that would convince him that he was truly himself by putting himself in direct contact with what was the ultimate reality in himself and also the ultimate reality in the universe. With great spiritual and intellectual heroism, he totally rejected his own artistic productions, including his epic novel *War and Peace,* as worthless. He scathingly, brutally criticized as did Dostoevsky inventions of European culture, philosophical, religious, artistic. He sought the renovation of Russia by inventing a new form of religion that unfortunately was not based on the discovery of his own spiritual personhood which tragically he never discovered. Somehow Russians of the 19th century when everything has been taken from them, or better, when circumstances have forced them to strip themselves of their own invention of themselves, when they reach a kind of spiritual and intellectual devastation — then they find in themselves a deep need to search for themselves by searching for the soul of Russia. Tolstoy at the very end of his life left his aristocratic mansion and began wandering alone on roads in search of whatever positive transformation might take place in him if he could press his feet down again and again on Russian soil wandering alone on strange roads. Stepan Trofimovich also in the end faces the truth of the meaninglessness of his life and abandons all like Tolstoy. He heads out alone on a road to nowhere hoping like Tolstoy that he will find a self, a true self, now that his life is nearly over, the true self that he never found by living as an inauthentic self in his phony marriage to Varvara Petrovna.

13

The narrator of the novel does not reveal his name until halfway through his story and before writes it as G —— — V. We know about him only that he has "a classical education" and that he is a close, intimate friend of Stepan Trofimovich. At moments of despair in his relationship with Varvara Petrovna, Stepan Trofimovich embraces him and cries tears onto his shoulder. He tells us what is going on in the town but reveals very selectively what is going on behind the scenes of regular society. When odd and strange events happen, he appears surprised and encourages us to be surprised along with him. He relates the plot somewhat like the narrator of a mystery novel. When the two antagonistic friends in a false marriage are back from their troubled time in Saint Petersburg, where they failed to connect with the new generation with new revolutionary ideas, he tells us "we had a period of stagnation which lasted nine years". We are told that Stepan Trofimovich has been the tutor of young Stavrogin as a child and that the two have left the young man behind at a lycee in Petersburg. Back from Petersburg, where Stepan Trofimovitch tried to reestablish himself as a leading revolutionary and failed, Varvara Petrovna allows her creation, Stepan Trofimovich, to live on her property in a separate house. He spends time at the local club playing and losing at cards. At his house, he and the narrator meet twice a week with a circle of friends. This serves to give us insight into some of the false apostles of Stavrogin, some of the local revolutionaries. They meet together each week. "We were a merry party," says the narrator, "especially when he was not sparing of the champagne." Stepan Trofimovich has given up his youthful ambition to be a serious writer and a serious revolutionary. Varvara Petrovna pays regularly for his losses at cards and the champagne and our narrator has the opportunity to gossip about the persons at Stepan Trofimovich's club or about those in the circle that meets at Stepan's house. He gives us quick sketches of characters that leave us wondering who they are really and what they might be up to. It is only later when we are moved deeply by the drama going on behind the scenes in a new underground with new underground men that we realize that some of the members of the circle are also secretly revolutionaries, members of a strange group of twelve apostles in reverse related to Stavrogin, a Christ in reverse.

Liputin is one of the first members of the circle. He is a provincial official and "was reputed in the town to be an atheist". He is a "scandal-monger" known for his "backbiting". He was married twice. He was "not much respected in the town, and was not received in the best circles". "Vavara Petrovna disliked him, but he always knew how to make up to her". Later in the story, when the revolutionary apostles are incited by Pyotr Stepanovich to murder Shatov, Liputin will be the Judas who betrays them to the authorities.

Shatov becomes a member of the circle during the last years of the nine-year period. We find out that he had also been a student of Stepan Trofimovich and that he had been expelled from the university. He went abroad as a tutor in a family and married a "free-thinking" young lady who was also a member of the household. They lived together three weeks in Geneva and parted "as free people recognizing no bonds". For a long time afterwards, Shatov wandered around Europe. Varvara Petrovna dislikes Shatov for his pride. He is the son of a former valet of hers and at his birth was her serf. She has brought up his sister Dasha. She was "a favorite of hers, and Varvara Petrovna treated her with respect and consideration in her house".

Virginsky, a quiet young man of considerable education is a member of the circle. He has a wife who "professed the very latest convictions". The circle of Stepan Trofimovich is rumored in the town to be "a hotbed of nihilism, profligacy and godlessness" although our narrator argues that the circle indulged only in "the most harmless, agreeable, typically Russian, light-hearted liberal chatter". After a year of marriage, Virginsky's wife announced to him "that he was superseded and that she preferred Lebyadkin". Virginsky, clearly trying to obey some revolutionary principle that did not derive from "light-hearted liberal chatter", tells his wife that before he only loved her but "now I respect you". Some in the circle believe Virginsky accepted that he was "superseded" with a renunciation "worthy of ancient Rome". Others say "that he wept violently". In any case, at a picnic shortly after he was "superseded", Virginsky threw to the wind any advanced principle about marriage he might have adhered to, seized the giant Lebyadkin, grabbed him by the hair and dragged him along the ground "with shrieks, shouts and tears". Lebyadkin, a stranger to the town, leaves town shortly afterward. Virginsky's wife refuses to forgive her husband. Then, after describing at length this outcome of the new principles, the narrator informs us in one sentence, almost as an unimportant aside, that Lebyadkin came back to town recently with his sister. This minor bit of gossip hides behind it unrevealed by the narrator a fact that when revealed will cause a heart-rending deep pain in the mind and soul of Varvara Petrovna: Lebyadkin's sister, Marya Timofyevna, is a cripple from the lowest class of society with a mad, deranged mind that her son Stavrogin has legally married. But information we get from Stepan Trofimovich's circle, a harmless and light-hearted gathering, does not reveal this and other strange and unnatural acts going on in their provincial society below the society's surface. Later they will punch holes in its normal well-ordered way of life.

But one night at the circle in the middle of the "light-hearted liberal chatter", Shatov does reveal the depth of his feelings for Slavophilism. Stepan Trofimovich, the central wit of the circle, gives the group his notions about God. "I believe in God, *mais distinguons,* I believe in Him as a Being who is conscious of Himself in me only. I cannot believe as my Natasha (the servant) or like some country gentleman who believes 'to be on the safe side,' or like our dear Shatov — but no, Shatov doesn't come into it, Shatov believes 'on principle', like a Moscow Slavophile. As for Christianity, for all my genuine respect for it, I'm not a Christian. I am more of an antique pagan, like the great Goethe, or like an ancient Greek." Shatov who is listening says nothing until Stepan Trofimovich talking on and on asserts with feeling that writers of the past like Gogol "knew how to love their people, they knew how to suffer for them…".

Then Shatov cannot contain himself and growls,

"Those men of yours never loved the people, they didn't suffer for them, and didn't sacrifice anything for them, though they may have amused themselves by imagining it." Then, after Stepan Trofimovich disagrees yelling, Shatov yells back, "You can't love what you don't know and they had no conception of the Russian people. All of them peered at the Russian people through their fingers, and you do too."

Shatov is twenty-eight, short, awkward with broad shoulders, thick lips. "His hair was always in a wild tangle and stood up in a shock which nothing could smooth." He has "a hostile, obstinately downcast, as it were shamefaced, expression in his eyes." He was raised in Varvara Petrovna's house with her son Stavrogin.

Stavrogin at twenty-five comes to the province after rumors have reached the town about his riotous living in Petersburg. He has drunk and gambled too much and lived savagely running over people in the streets with his horses. He insulted a lady of good society with whom he had a liaison and has bullied and insulted people for the mere pleasure of insulting them. He was an army officer but fought two duels for which he was to blame. He killed one man and maimed the other. He was degraded to the ranks as punishment but quickly rose to the rank of an officer. Back in Petersburg, he resigned his commission in the army and began dressing in rags associating with the dregs of society living in dark slums and all sorts of low haunts. We find out later that both Kirillov and Shatov live side by side with Stavrogin in these lowest depths of society. The three have intense discussions about various subjects. An aristocrat with money and social rank thus chooses to live in the underground of Petersburg and acts willfully like the man from the underground. For Dostoevsky the unrelenting law of his religion is that any life grounded in anything but God becomes godless and worthless. Freedom is at the bottom of everything and it must lead either to nothingness or to God. Stavrogin's nothingness does not keep him living with the dregs of society. His nothingness can also enslave him even when he chooses to live at the top of society. When he appears for the first time in the provincial society of his mother, Varvara Petrovna, he is elegant and well-dressed. He has the air and manner of a man accustomed to culture and refinement. "His hair was of a peculiarly intense black, his light-colored eyes were peculiarly light and calm, his complexion was peculiarly soft and white, the red in his cheeks was too bright and clear, his teeth were like pearls, and his lips like coral — one would have thought that he must be a paragon of beauty, yet at the same time there seemed something repellent about him." Shatov, the peasant trying to root his life in love of the Russian people, hates and loves this soulless aristocrat who can not love anything including the Russian people. While living in the province among regular society, Stavrogin's demon comes to the surface. One day at the provincial club, he grasps the nose of one of the club's most respected members and pulls him two or three steps across a room in full view of club members. On another occasion in society, he begins kissing a pretty married woman in the presence of her husband. In his final act of willfulness, he bites the ear of the province's governor. Another underground man rises to the surface and acts willfully.

Stavrogin is judged to have acted as he did because of some mental sickness with a physical origin. He leaves the provincial town and travels abroad for three years. Just before his return to the province, his mother has both positive and negative news about him. He has kept company abroad with a girl of an upper class family, Lisaveta Nikolaevna, and there is reason to believe that their engagement will soon be announced. But Varvara Petrovna has also heard from gossip about the province and from anonymous letters that Stavrogin has been sending money to Lebyadkin to help him maintain his crippled, mad sister, Marya Timofyevna. Varvara Petrovna encounters the crippled young woman leaving church on a Sunday and brings her to her house. She is determined to uncover the details of her son's relationship to her. Many of the main characters are present in the main room of her house as she questions the girl: the narrator, Stepan Trofimovich, Shatov and his sister Dasha, Lisaveta Nikolaevna and her mother. Lebyadkin, the brother of the crippled girl, Marya Timofyevna, arrives and is shown into the main room where he is questioned intensely by Varvara Petrovna. He succeeds in not revealing that his sister is in fact legally married to her son Stavrogin. It is a long dramatic scene. Finally, Stavrogin arrives at his mother's house back from his trip abroad and enters the scene. His mother asks him directly if he is married to the cripple, Marya Timofyevna. He does not answer her directly. Instead, he goes to the cripple and talks to her sympathetically. Then he escorts her out of the room. Pyotor Stepanovich Verhovensky, Stepan Trofimovich's son, the leader of the secret revolutionary group of false apostles devoted to the false Christ, Stavrogin, arrives on the scene after Stavrogin has left with his wife, Lebyadkin's crippled sister. He ingratiates himself with Varvara Petrovna by a long detailed story about Stavrogin and the crippled young woman. He explains that Stavrogin has been giving her money simply out of the goodness of his heart because she is in need. Varvara Petrovna has been in a distressed state of mind because she has faced as a real possibility the terrible truth that her son is legally married to the cripple. She believes with her whole heart the false explanation of Pyotor Stepanovich and becomes so ecstatic with happiness that she actually recognizes, carried away by her effusive and unrealistic praise of her son, whom we see as a false Christ, that his actions in relation to the cripple are "holy". She uses the Russian for "holy", "svjatoj" twice. She says about her son's kindly relationship with the crippled young woman, "No, it was something higher than eccentricity, and I assure you, something holy even." Shortly after, she asks Pyotor Stepanovich, "Can you really refuse to recognize the lofty compassion, the noble tremor of the whole organism with which Nicolas answered Kirillov, 'I do not laugh at her'! A noble, holy answer!" No doubt the mother of the real Christ also considered her son's actions holy but they were true and not falsified as in Pyotor Stepanovich's lying story. Stavrogin's possible future fiancee, Lisaveta Nikolaevna, listens to the talk very nervously and becomes hysterical. But she is attended to and calmed. Finally, when the long complicated scene is near its end, Stavrogin returns to the room. Shatov, who has been sitting in the room silently during all the talk, stands up and walks to Stavrogin. He stands before him and punches him with all his might on the left side of his face making blood immediately spurt from his mouth. Shatov turns and leaves. Lisaveta Nikolaevna faints and her head hits the floor as she falls with a thud.

14

Eight days pass. The provincial society buzzes with excited nervous energy about what will happen next.

Stavrogin has killed a man in a duel and all are wondering whether he will kill Shatov. Then late on a rainy night we follow along with Stavrogin as he leaves his home and walks through muddy streets. Previously most of the novel has been related to us bit by bit superficially by our narrator. He gives us all kinds of gossip about what is going on but it does not satisfy us. We feel a need to know finally what is going on really. What is the drama building to? What will be the obligatory scene that will make what has happened previously meaningful? The dramatic punch to the face of Stavrogin by Shatov makes us sure that we will get finally to the crucial place where the drama is heading. We follow along with Stavrogin walking in the mud feeling deeply ill at ease and fearful but somehow certain that something powerful must happen caused by this devilish young aristocrat going somewhere in the darkness of a rainy night.

If Stavrogin is a false Christ, if he has grown up with a false father in a non-marriage marriage with his mother, if his real father is mysteriously absent, if a Peter, Pyotor Stepanovich. is diabolically devoted to him and leading for him a group of false disciples, then a possible obligatory scene would be a false religious conversion of one of his false disciples. But how can Stavrogin convert a man either falsely or truly if there is no holiness within him and instead a diabolical nothingness?

The character of the real Christ can not be understood because within him is the unfathomable being of the godhead. Christ can be believed and loved but he can be known only by ourselves actually becoming in our being like him. To believe in Christ really means to no longer believe in one's own self. My attachment to Christ spiritually means for me to become other than myself by actually uniting with the godhead in him. It is not a question of knowing him with my mind but of becoming myself Christ in my soul. Stavrogin even as a false Christ resembles the real Christ because he also has a character that can not be known. It is impossible to say "Stavrogin is this kind of man" because he is not like any man. He is a mystery to himself and those who try and fail to relate to him never know who he is. But the less they are able to understand who he is, the more they wish to relate to him and failing this they end, influenced by the nothingness within him, by becoming nothing themselves. Dasha, the sister of Shatov, is a willing prisoner of Stavrogin. She confesses to him that she will follow him anywhere and devote herself to him for her whole life. But it is impossible for a woman to fall in love with such a man in a normal way. Lisaveta Nikolaevna becomes hysterical in his presence, faints and hits her head against the floor. He is simply not a man with some regular recognizable character. Dostoevsky, who regularly read the New Testament, knew in his being the real Christ and it taught him that another living imitation of a man could be created who might walk among men with a nothingness within him that was as unknowable as the godhead in Christ. Christ had to imitate a man because he was not only a man. With Stavrogin, Dostoevsky did the impossible. This great creator of hundreds of characters clearly knowable by detail after detail of their individual beings finally created a believable Christ-like person unknowable to himself and totally unknowable to the characters around him who are diabolically drawn to him. Stavrogin is a Christ without a godhead. He is a sham imitation of a real man and of a real God.

In one scene Stavrogin says to Kirillov wrathfully, "I

can't understand anything now. Why does everyone expect of me something not expected from anyone else? Why am I to put up with what no one else puts up with, and undertake burdens no one else can bear?"

"I thought you were seeking a burden for yourself."

"I seek a burden?"

"Yes."

"You've... seen that?"

"Yes."

"Is it so noticeable?"

"Yes."

Stavrogin's disciples all want him to lighten the burden in their lost souls by leading them somewhere to some place where they are incapable of going by themselves. He in turn feels a burden placed upon him by them but he will not lead them because at the bottom of his soul he is nothing and he has no place to go to feel at home either in himself or in the world of men. When he leaves his house this night to visit Kirillov and Shatov, it is cold and wet and he walks in the darkness with his boots reaching down step after step into the mud. A false Christ's path through the night and the mud is as full of darkness as the real Christ's was full of light. In fact, after the dramatic punch in the face he received from Shatov, we have a heightened sense of fear that something terrible is about to happen. We have the deep impression because Stavrogin is so mysterious and so strange that he is the devil himself out walking alone in the night and about to pull from the darkness into our hearts evil.

Stavrogin visits Kirillov who lives in a house next to Shatov's house on Bogoyavlensky Street. The two young men talk. Stavrogin has come because he must fight a duel the next day with a man named Gaganov. He wants

Kirillov to be his second and arrange the details of the duel. Kirillov agrees to do it and shows the duelling pistols he possesses that they can use. Then we learn through their talk of the dire influence that Stavrogin has had on Kirillov.

"Whose baby was that just now?" asks Stavrogin.

"The old woman's mother-in-law is here — no, daughter-in-law, it's all the same. Three days. She's lying ill with the baby, it cries a lot at night, it's the stomach. The mother sleeps, but the old woman picks it up; I play ball with it. The ball's from Hamburg. I bought it in Hamburg to throw it and catch it, it strengthens the spine. It's a girl."

"Are you fond of children?"

"'I am,' answered Kirilov, though rather indifferently."

"Then, you're fond of life?"

"Yes, I'm fond of life! What of it?"

"Though you've made up your mind to shoot yourself?"

"What of it? Why connect it? Life's one thing and that's another. Life exists, but death doesn't at all."

"You've begun to believe in a future eternal life?"

"No, not in a future eternal life, but in eternal life here. There are moments, you reach moments, and time suddenly stands still, and it will become eternal."

"You hope to reach such a moment?"

"Yes."

"'That'll scarcely be possible in our time,' Stavrogin responded slowly and, as it were, dreamily; the two spoke without the slightest irony. 'In the Apocalypse the angel swears that there will be no time.'"

"I know. That's very true, distinct and exact. When all mankind attains happiness then there will be no more time, for there'll be no need of it — a very true thought."

"Where will they put it?"

"Nowhere. Time's not an object but an idea. It will be extinguished in the mind."

It is night on Bogoyavlensky Street and with two Russians talking strangely we discover finally what Dostoevsky's great work is about. It is that absent from ordinary life extraordinary human experiences can happen. For a third of his novel he has been painting for us, through the pleasant and objective description of his narrator, regular and ordinary life in provincial Russia. Almost everything happens ordinarily and little happens of much importance except that we have hints here and there that something quite unordinary is going on behind the external scenes. The revolutionaries that Stepan Trofimovich and Varvara Petrovna have met in St Petersburg are unusual and disturbing. The two can not adjust to the new ideas and retreat back home to the secure and ordinary life in their province. Shatov speaks boldly and angrily about his love for the Russian people and about the superficiality of Stepan Trofimovich and Russians who falsely claim they love the people. The bits of information about Stavrogin's life away from the provincial society are disturbing because of his willfulness and brutality and his crazy antisocial acts when he returns to the provincial society are also disturbing but his actions are explained away by a physical sickness as the cause of his madness. We find out that in Switzerland he may have started a relationship with Lisaveta Nikolaevna that might lead to a regular marriage. Then anonymous letters reach Varvara that her son may be married to a crippled girl. Marya Timofyevna arrives at church one Sunday and Varvara Petrovna takes her home and interviews her and her brother Lebyadkin to try to find out if there is truth to what has been revealed to her anonymously in letters. But her son arrives on the scene in his mother's house, takes the crippled girl away to her home, and his lying disciple, Pyotor Stepanovich, ingratiates himself with Varvara Petrovna and covers over the extraordinary marriage of her son to a cripple with lies. Everything goes back to normal except that Lisaveta Nikolaevna faints and Shatov, silent throughout the long scene, walks across the room and punches Stavrogin in the face. Some unusual things are happening like the sudden punch from Shatov and Lisaveta Nikolaevna's fainting, but in general everything seems normal and regular. Except that the normal and the regular do not interest Dostoevsky. His business is creating Raskolnikovs and men from the underground where nothing is normal and regular. Now it is night. Stavrogin has left the security of his home and we must face with him in the darkness things that do not take place in the regular light of ordinary days.

"You seem to be very happy, Kirillov," says Stavrogin.

"Yes. very happy."

"When did you find out you were so happy?"

"Last week, on Tuesday — no, Wednesday, for it was Wednesday by that time, in the night."

"By what reasoning?"

"I don't remember. I was walking about the room; never mind, I stopped my clock. It was thirty-seven minutes past two."

"As an emblem of the fact that there will be no more time?"

Kirillov was silent a moment.

"Men are bad because they don't know they're good... They'll find out that they're good and they'll all become good, everyone of them."

"Here you've found it out, so have you become good then?"

"I am good….He who teaches that all are good will end the world."

"He who taught it was crucified."

"He will come, and his name will be the man-god."

"The god-man?"

"The man-god. That's the difference."

"Surely it wasn't you who lit the lamp under the ikon?"

"Yes, it was I who lit it."

"Did you do it believing?"

"The old woman likes to have the lamp and she hadn't time to do it today."

"You don't say prayers yourself?"

"I pray to everything. You see the spider crawling on the wall? I look at it and thank it for crawling."

"I bet that when I come next time you'll be believing in God too."

Stavrogin got up and took his hat.

"Why?"

"If you were to find out that you believe in God, then you'd believe in Him; but since you don't know that you believe in Him, then you don't believe in Him," said Stavrogin with a laugh.

"That's not right. You've distorted the idea. It's a flippant joke. Remember what you have meant in my life, Stavrogin."

"Good-bye, Kirillov."

This strange talk between two men about going beyond time or existing without time is where Dostoevsky is now taking us. He is going to try to take us where Kirillov spoke of being, to "eternal life here". "There are moments," Kirilov has said, " you reach moments, and time suddenly stands still, and it will become eternal." "You hope to reach such a moment?"asks Stavrogin. "Yes," says Kirillov. Can we reach such a moment? If we reach a moment beyond time what will we find? We do not know and we do not know if Dostoevsky knew. But the scene that follows between Stavrogin and Shatov does have some strange quality about it, some power of creative inspiration from Dostoevsky that gives us moments reading it that do take us beyond time. But Dostoevsky introduces in their talk a new element that his inspiration tells him is necessary for travellers trying to reach beyond time, love. What is beyond time is love but the time that rules our lives does not allow this love to exist. The love that we know, the ordinary love that exists among men and women, the only love that time allows us to accept as real, this type of love is totally destroyed among couples in his novel. Vavara keeps Stepan in economic and emotional slavery to her and finally breaks their loveless relationship completely. Shatov has married and his wife has left him. Lisaveta and Stavrogin can not love one another even though she is passionately drawn to him and gives herself to him hurting deeply the honor of another man who is courting her, the strong and honest Mavriky Nikolaevich. Lisaveta experiences "outbreaks of blind hatred for Mavriky". She esteems Mavriky and loves him but she has nonetheless towards him "a peculiar unconscious hatred which at times she could not control". Julia von Lembke, the wife of the governor of the province, constantly belittles the governor and finally drives him crazy so that he must retreat to a sanatorium in Switzerland to try to recover. Stavrogin has secretly married the crippled girl Marya Timofyevna and they have no normal relationship.

So like his mother and Stepan Trofimovich, he has also created a marriage that, even though legal, is a false marriage since it has never been consummated, This kind of love for Dostoevsky, regular human love, leads nowhere. The Underground Man throws away the love of a woman. Raskolnikov can not escape his rational madness and join with Sonya in the secret place within her where she lives. But Dostoevsky now tries to take us to another kind of love, to a divine love located in a secret place beyond time.

15

Stavrogin enters the house next to Kirillov's house where Shatov lives. He finds himself in total darkness. He gropes around to find the stairs up to Shatov's room when a door opens above on the top landing. A light shines from it. Shatov had pushed open the door without coming out. Dostoevsky thus gives us his message quickly and unmistakably. Stavrogin lives in darkness and the light above that Shatov displays to him is what he needs. Stavrogin climbs the stairs and finds Shatov standing back in a corner of the room, Then he takes away any idea that he has come for any purpose related to a need for light or spiritual discovery. He tells Shatov he has come on business.

He uses the word that is the common, everyday word of Russians for practical down-to-earth business, *delo*. Shatov is in no mood for such business. He has shut himself up in his room for eight days. When the narrator of the novel came to his room to visit him, he yelled at him from behind his locked door that he would not open it. He invites Stavrogin to have a seat at a table and is confused about who should shut the door. He tells Stavrogin to do it and then instead closes it himself. He has grown thinner and is in a fever. He sits at the table opposite Stavrogin.

"You've been worrying me to death," says Shatov, "looking down, in a soft half-whisper. 'Why didn't you come?'"

"You were so sure that I'd come, then?"

"Yes; wait a minute, I have been delirious...perhaps I'm delirious now...Wait a minute."

Shatov's state is feverish and delirious. This contrasts with Stavrogin's state of calm which is centered in some need to talk business. Shatov gets up and takes a revolver from the top of three shelves of books.

"One night, in delirium, I fancied that you were coming to kill me, and early next morning I spent my last ruble on buying a revolver from that good-for-nothing fellow Lyamshin; I did not mean to let you do it. Then I came to myself again...I've neither powder nor shot; it has been lying there on the shelf till now; wait a minute…"

Stavrogin still calm brings up the subject of why Shatov punched him.

"You didn't give me that blow because of my affair with your wife?"

""You know I didn't yourself,' said Shatov, looking down again."

"'Then I guessed right and you too guessed right,"'Stavrogin went on in a tranquil voice. 'You are right. Marya Timofyevna Lebyadkin is my lawful wife, married to me four and a half years ago in Petersburg. I suppose the blow was on her account?'

Shatov, utterly astounded, listened in silence.

'I guessed but did not believe it,' he muttered at last, looking strangely at Stavrogin.

'And you struck me?'

Shatov flushed and mumbled almost incoherently:

'Because of your fall...your lie. I didn't go up to you to punish you...I didn't know when I went up to you that I should strike you. I did it because you meant so much in my life...I...'

'I understand. I understand, be careful about what you say. I am sorry you are feverish. I've come about a most urgent matter.'"

But Stavrogin does not understand. He again uses the word for practical business. Shatov is mentally and spiritually far beyond any business that is merely practical. He does not know what exactly his business with Stavrogin is although he knows it started a few years ago in their Petersburg days. Stavrogin had talked to him then about Christianity as though it were a subject that he took deeply and seriously. The handsome aristocrat had abandoned his place in high society and had chosen to live with Kirillov and himself in poverty in the slums of St. Petersburg. In those days, as Stavrogin had talked on one occasion, Shatov had sensed something in Stavrogin's being that did not belong to his usual and ordinary being. His words were powerful spiritually and they brought to life in Shatov's being something he himself had never sensed was there. Yes, it seemed to Shatov that there was a *secret place* in Stavrogin just as in Sonya. This secret place that Shatov sensed in Stavrogin was beginning to reveal itself to him as he listened to his aristocratic friend tell him that he thought Russians were a god-bearing people and that the Russian God alive within the Russian people was like the river of life that Saint John had written about in the Apocalypse. Another man was speaking to him man to man about the mystery of God and revealing the existence of God in himself. Suddenly from some mysterious secret place God was revealing himself to two men and joining them spiritually by something that felt like a spiritual love. It was a beautiful, inspiring experience for Shatov unlike anything he had ever known. It touched him so deeply that it changed his being, his self, forever. Now more than two years later Shatov wants to find again the being within Stavrogin that changed his own being so deeply during those days together in Petersburg. It must still exist now in Stavrogin if it existed then. He was then almost like a Christ meeting with a common everyday man and turning him by the divinity that shone forth from his being as he spoke into a fervent believer in God and an apostle of his teaching. But was Stavrogin a Christ that day for Shatov or was it just talk that came from Stavrogin's groundlessness and was merely something that on that day happened to amuse him to talk about?

Those words that came from him two years before in their days together in Petersburg became necessary spiritually for Shatov. He has just said to Stavrogin, "I did it because you meant so much in my life...I..." When he walked across the crowded room eight days ago in the drawing room of Varvara Petrovna, Stavrogin's mother, towards her son, Shatov has just said about it, "I didn't know when I went up to you that I should strike you". But he did know that "you meant so much in my life" and that he had to have something to do directly with a being that had meant so much to him because he has seen his "fall" and his "lie". He says he struck him "because of your fall...your lie". Could it be that he walked across the room to save Stavrogin's soul and the soul that Stavrogin had awakened in himself? Could it be that the punch in the face that he delivered to his degraded friend was an act of love? Whatever it was, Stavrogin does not understand even though he says, "I understand. I understand."

"'I have been expecting you too long.' Shatov seemed to be quivering all over, and he got up from his seat. 'Say what you have to say...I'll speak too...later.'"

The business that Stavrogin has come to talk about is his knowledge that the group of revolutionaries may murder Shatov. Shatov says he is aware that his life may be in danger but it is not this "business" of Stavrogin's that interests him. He has already not reacted practically and reasonably when Stavrogin just confirmed that he was married to the cripple Marya Timofyevna. Shatov says he guessed it was true. "I guessed but did not believe it," he muttered. "And you struck me?" asks Stavrogin. "Shatov flushed and mumbled almost incoherently: 'Because of your fall...your lie. I didn't go up to you to punish you...I didn't know when I went up to you that I should strike you... I did it because you meant so much in my life...I...'" It is not something that Shatov can explain in practical language to Stavrogin. It is never on Shatov's part in this conversation ever simply about some business. It is about his relationship with Stavrogin. He must confront Stavrogin to try to reach the reality of their relationship on some super personal level even if he does not understand clearly where he is going or where he will arrive. And at this moment in their dialogue, Shatov dismisses Stavrogin's warning that his life is in danger as simply some unimportant matter that he does not care about. In fact, throughout their talk he does not react realistically to what Stavrogin says. He is in a fever. He is delirious. Stavrogin has meant so much to him. He has waited for him for so long. His Messiah, his Christ is sitting across the table from him and talking business and Shatov continually tries to reach some business that he has with Stavrogin's being that is beyond time.

Yet Shatov does have a practical question for Stavrogin. When he gets an answer it drives him again to some place in his mind and emotions that is at a much deeper level than anything Stavrogin thinks or feels.

"'I know that I may be in some danger,' he said in measured tones, 'but how can you have come to know of it?'

'Because I belong to them as you do, and am a member of their society, just as you are.'

'You...you are a member of the society?'

'I see from your eyes that you were prepared for anything from me rather than that,' said Stavrogin with a faint smile. 'But, excuse me, you knew that there would be an attempt on your life?'

'Nothing of the sort. And I don't think so now, in spite of your words.

Though...though there's no being sure of anything with these fools!'"

They discuss the secret revolutionary society. We learn that Shatov joined the society two years ago before a trip to America. We learn that in America his views changed after the fatal conversation the two had had living in poverty in Petersburg before Shatov left. This conversation that took place in Petersburg inspired Shatov to write a long six-page letter to Stavrogin from America. Their conversation had changed Shatov's ideas fatally and set him on a path away from his socialist ideas towards belief in Christianity. It is this influence on him by the ideas that Stavrogin expressed to him about Christianity that inspires Shatov now to probe Stavrogin to find out if he still believes what he said then. We learn also that Stavrogin sent Shatov the money he needed to come back from America to Russia. Once these details are out in the open, we come back to the powerful reaction of Shatov when he finds out that Stavrogin, his Christ, his exalted friend who once spoke divine words about the truths of Christianity, has joined the group of revolutionaries.

"'You, you, Stavrogin, how could you mix yourself up with such shameful, stupid, second-hand absurdity? You a member of the society? What an exploit for Stavrogin!' he cried suddenly, in despair.

He clasped his hands, as though nothing could be a bitterer and a more inconsolable grief to him than such a discovery.

'Excuse me," said Stavrogin, extremely surprised, 'but you seem to look upon me as a sort of sun, and on yourself as an insect in comparison. I noticed that even from your letter in America.'"

They talk about Stavrogin's marriage to the cripple Marya Timofyevna. Stavrogin shocks Shatov by revealing that he plans to soon make it public and by telling him also that his wife of more than four years is still a virgin. We have here again in a distorted fashion the comparison of the false Christ to the real Christ. Another Mary, Marya Timofyevna, a woman like Mary, the mother of God, who is married but is a virgin. A man, a kind of superman like Christ, who can only imitate life and not live it as a normal man, and so he makes a false marriage, an imitation of marriage with a cripple who is still a virgin. Shatov is shocked by the talk of Marya. "Shatov hid his face in his hand, turned away, but suddenly clutched Stavrogin by the shoulders.

'Do you know why, do you know why, anyway,' he shouted, 'why you did all this, and why you are resolved on such a punishment now?'

'Your question is clever and malignant, but I mean to

surprise you too; I fancy I do know why I got married then, and why I am resolved on such a punishment now as you express it.'

'Let's leave that...of that later. Put it off. Let's talk of the chief thing, the chief thing. I've been waiting two years for you.'

'Yes?'

'I've waited too long for you. I've been thinking of you incessantly. You are the only man who could move ...I wrote to you about it from America.'

'I remember your long letter very well.'

'Too long to read? No doubt; six sheets of paper. Don't speak! Don't speak! Tell me, can you spare me another ten minutes?... But now, this minute... I have waited for you too long.'

'Certainly, half an hour if you like, but not more, if that will suit you.'

'And on condition, too,' Shatov put in angrily, 'that you take a different tone. Do you hear? I'm demanding when I should be imploring. Do you understand what it means to demand when one ought to implore?'

'I understand that in that way you lift yourself above all ordinary considerations for the sake of loftier aims,' Stavrogin said with a faint smile. 'I see with regret, too, that you're feverish.'

'I beg you to treat me with respect, I insist on it!' Shatov shouted, 'Not respect for me personally — to hell with that — — but something else, just for this once. While I am talking... we are two beings, and have come together in infinity... for the last time in the world. Drop your tone, and speak like a human being! Speak, if only for once in your life, with the voice of a man. I say it not for my sake but for yours. Do you understand that you ought to forgive me that blow in the face if only because I gave you the opportunity of realizing your immense power?...Ah, again you smile your disdainful, worldly smile! Ah, when will you understand me! Have done with being a snob! Understand that I insist on that! I insist on it, else I won't speak, I'm not going to for anything!'

His excitement was approaching frenzy. Stavrogin frowned and seemed to grow more careful.

'Since I am remaining another half-hour with you when time is so precious ,' he pronounced earnestly and impressively, 'you may be assured that I mean to listen to you at least with interest...and I am convinced that I will hear from you much that is new.'

He sat down on a chair.

'Sit down!' Shatov shouted, abruptly throwing himself into his chair too."

Shatov speaks to him threateningly with flashing eyes. He says that there is only one god-bearing nation on earth and asks Stavrogin if he knows what nation he is referring to. Stavrogin answers that he has no choice by the way Shatov is speaking except to answer the Russian nation. Shatov says he is already laughing and Stavrogin answers that he expected he would say "something like that". Shatov repeats intensely as a question, "Something like that? And don't you know those words yourself?" Stavrogin admits they are familiar, that the words "god-bearing nation" were simply the conclusion of a conversation they had two years ago shortly before Shatov left for the United States. We will see as their talk proceeds that Shatov will repeat to Stavrogin the very words Stavrogin spoke to him in that fatal conversation. Here he will not let Stavrogin get by saying it was a conversation.

"It's your phrase altogether, not mine," says Shatov. " Your own and not the conclusion of some conversation we had. There was no conversation between us. It was a teacher saying great words and a disciple who was raised from the dead. I was that disciple and you were the teacher.."

The reference to Christ and the raising of Lazarus indicates again Dostoevsky's intention of creating in Stavrogin a false Christ and it foreshadows the false conversion of his disciple, Shatov, which is soon to happen. Another indication of the presence of a false Christ is Shatov demanding of the mysterious person before him that he "speak like a human being". Then he emphasises that Stavrogin like the real Christ is an imitation of a man by demanding, "Speak, if only for once in your life, with the voice of a man." Shatov is not the only one who recognizes the mysterious, inhuman personhood that Dostoevsky has constructed inside Stavrogin. Just two or three hours before, shortly before Stavrogin leaves his house, his mother knocks on the door of his room. She receives no answer and opens the door. "Seeing that Nikolai Vsyevolodovich was sitting strangely motionless, she cautiously advanced to the sofa with a throbbing heart. She seemed struck by the fact that he could fall asleep so quickly and that he could sleep sitting like that, so erect and motionless, so that his breathing even was scarcely perceptible. His face was pale and forbidding, but it looked, as it were, numb and rigid. His brows were somewhat contracted and frowning. He positively had the look of a lifeless wax figure. She stood over him for about three minutes, almost holding her breath, and suddenly she was seized with terror. She withdrew on tiptoe, stopped at the door, hurriedly made the sign of the cross over him, and retreated unobserved, with a new oppression and a new anguish in her heart." Shatov is therefore not the only one who perceives the strange, inhuman character of Stavrogin. But he was once at the most important moments in Shatov's life "a teacher saying great words" and he himself like Lazarus in the gospel was "a disciple who was raised from the dead". Shatov now wants with his whole soul to repeat the very words Stavrogin said to him two years before in order to raise himself again from the dead and Stavrogin along with him. He will repeat Stavrogin's words with such accuracy and such passion that indeed that is his intention. But Dostoevsky's genius will extract an opposite result than the one we expect. The very words of the real Christ raised his disciples from spiritual death. The very words of the false Christ sitting before Shatov will raise Shatov from spiritual death not by the discovery that the words are true and genuine but by the revelation that they are false and worthless because coming from an empty and sinful soul.

Stavrogin answers that just after their talk that day that Shatov joined the revolutionary society and then left for America. Shatov agrees with him and says that he wrote to him about it from America. He says, "It is difficult to change Gods. I did not believe you then, because I did not want to believe, I plunged for the last time into that sewer... But the seed remained and grew up. Seriously, tell me seriously, didn't you read all of my letter from America, perhaps you didn't read it all?"

"I read three pages of it. The two first and the last. And I glanced through the middle as well. But I was always meaning …"

"'Ah, never mind, drop it! Damn it!' cried Shatov, waving his hand. 'If you've renounced those words about the people now, how could you have uttered them then?...That's what crushes me now.'

'I wasn't joking with you then; in persuading you I was perhaps more concerned with myself than with you,' Stavrogin pronounced enigmatically."

Whatever his intentions, he has planted a "seed" in Shatov that "grew up". But what will Shatov do with this seed that is still in him, the seed of belief in the Christian religion even though it has a nationalistic, Russian, slavophil side? Stavrogin has said he was not "joking".

"You weren't joking!" says Shatov. "In America I was lying on straw for three months beside a hapless creature, and I learnt from him that at the very time when you were sowing the seed of God and the Fatherland in my heart, at that very time, perhaps during those very days, you were infecting the heart of that hapless creature, that maniac Kirillov, with poison ...you confirmed false malignant ideas in him, and brought him to the verge of insanity...Go, look at him now, he is your creature...you've seen him though."

Stavrogin counters by saying he has just left Kirillov downstairs only a few moments ago and that he assured him that he was happy and good. He admits that Shatov's assumption that he was influencing Kirillov and him at about the same time is almost correct. But he insists he was not deceiving them. However the seed that was planted in Shatov seemed to Shatov a religious seed. He has to deal with that seed. That seed has been growing in him. He must dig into the being of the man who implanted it in him and find out what he was intending.

"Are you an atheist?" asks Shatov. "An atheist now?"
"Yes".
"And then?"

"Just as I was then."

They talk briefly about the respect they have for one another. Shatov interrupts him.

"Do you remember your expression," Shatov asks. "that 'an atheist can't be a Russian', that 'an atheist at once ceases to be Russian'? Do you remember saying that?"

"'Did I?' Stavrogin questioned him back.

'You ask? You've forgotten? And yet that was one of the truest statements of the leading peculiarity of the Russian soul, which you divined. You can't have forgotten it! I will remind you of something else. You said then that, 'a man who was not orthodox cannot be a Russian.'

'I imagine that's a slavophile idea.'

'The Slavophiles of today disown it. Nowadays, people have grown cleverer. But you went further: you believed that Roman Catholicism was not Christianity; you asserted that Rome proclaimed Christ subject to the third temptation of the devil. Announcing to all the world that Christ without an earthly kingdom cannot hold his ground upon earth, Catholicism by so doing proclaimed Antichrist and ruined the whole Western world...That's what you could say then! I remember our conversations.'

'If I believed it still, I'm sure I'd repeat it now. I wasn't lying when I spoke as though I was a believer.' Stavrogin speaks very seriously. 'But I assure you that recalling my former beliefs like this leaves an unpleasant aftertaste in my mouth, so I'd appreciate if you'd drop it. Could you manage that, do you think?'"

But Shatov will not drop it. He must continue pounding against Stavrogin's soul the very words he once said to him as though coming from Stavrogin's soul. Shatov *must* reach Stavrogin's soul or else he will never find out for sure whether the words of Stavrogin that touched his soul were real or not. But what will he feel in his soul when he finds out the truth? He does not know but he goes on anyway, relentlessly.

"If you believed it still!" cries Shatov. He completely ignores Stavrogin's request. "Wasn't it you who said that even if it was proved to you mathematically that the truth was outside of Christ, you would prefer to remain with Christ outside the truth? Did you say that? Did you?"

"Wait now. Let me ask you a question in my turn." Stavrogin answers raising his voice somewhat. "What, really, is the point of this impatient and hostile examination?"

"This examination is just about to be over for all eternity and you'll never be bothered with it again as long as you live."

"You keep insisting that we're outside the limits of time and space."

"Shut up!" shouts Shatov suddenly. "I know I'm stupid and awkward — and may my name be drowned in ridicule! Won't you allow me to repeat your leading idea to you? Only a few words — only the conclusion!"

"If it's only the conclusion, go ahead — repeat it."

Shatov leans forward in his chair. He raises his index finger. He is about to repeat the exact words that once touched his soul so deeply that he remembers them now more than two years later exactly.

"Not one single nation," he begins, as though reading it line by line, gazing menacingly at Stavrogin. "has, as yet, based its life on reason and science, except for a few moments, and then out of sheer stupidity. In its very essence, socialism is godless — it proclaimed in its very first statement that it aims at an organization that does not presuppose God; that is, an organization based on the principles of reason and science exclusively. But reason and science have always performed, and still perform, only an auxiliary function in the life of peoples, and it will be like that till the end of time. Nations are formed and moved by some other force whose origin is unknown and unaccountable. That force is the unquenchable will to reach an end and, at the same time, the denial of that end. It is the force of an incessant and unwavering affirmation of life and a denial of death. It is the spirit of life, 'river of water of life' as the Scriptures call it, the drying up of which is threatened in the Apocalypse. Some philosophers claim it is based on an aesthetic, others on an ethical principle, but I call it simply the search for God. The objective of any nationalist movement in any people in any time is actually a search for God, for their own, national God — and it must, above all, be their own God — and belief in Him as the only true God. God's personality is a synthesis of the entire nation from the beginning of its existence to its end. Never have all nations — or even many of them — shared one common God; each of them has always had its own God. When Gods become common, it is a sign that nations are doomed to disappear. When Gods are shared, they die; and belief in them dies as the nations disappear. The more vital a people, the more individual and special its god. There has never yet existed a people without religion — that is, without a concept of good and evil. Each nation has its own concept of good and evil and its own native good and evil. When many nations begin to have common concepts of good and evil, those nations die out and then the difference between good and evil starts to fade and vanishes. Reason has never had the power to define good and evil or even distinguish between them, if only approximately. On the contrary, reason has always mixed them up shamefully and miserably. As for science, its answers have always been based on brute force. This is particularly characteristic of the half-truths of science, the most terrible scourge of humanity, a scourge worse than plague, famine and war, an evil that didn't exist until this century. Half-truth is a tyrant without precedent, one that has its own priests and slaves; a tyrant that is worshiped with unprecedented awe and adulation and before which science itself fawns and cringes. Well, those are your own words, Stavrogin, except for the remark about half-truth; that's my own because I am myself a case of half-knowledge and that's why I hate it particularly. But I haven't modified any of your thoughts or even changed a word of what you said."

Who is the teacher now and who the disciple? The disciple, Shatov, is now teaching the teacher with the teacher's words that have become his own. These words touched him once deeply even though there is nothing about what he has just said or what he has said before that is truly religious like words from holy scripture. When he reminded Stavrogin that he said that "even if it was proved to you mathematically that the Truth was outside of Christ, you would prefer to remain with Christ outside the Truth" that was religious because it is nearly a paraphrase of the deep sentiments about Christ of Saint Paul. But these present words of Stavrogin, repeated by Shatov, are what one German critic called them, "religious prating". They are powerful, slavophil, nationalist words tying together religious hopes of a non-believer to hopes of power gained by transferring religious hopes to a fervent national pride. But these words nonetheless seeped into Shatov's being and took root there as a foreign seed planted in him by another man. Something has entered his being and taken it over and here we have the full genius of Dostoevsky at work and the exact meaning of this his greatest novel. *All the persons in his great novel are false persons.* All of them have had their very own self taken over and controlled by some alien power that they themselves are now powerless to even see as alien. Their own being is alien to them and they are always working diligently trying to make themselves comfortable with a sense of themselves that does not come from themselves. They are all possessed. Even if there is no devil, the concept of some devilish power within us taking control of our being is true. For Dostoevsky a seed has been planted in all of us that we must somehow seize and grab and pull out of our being and this is why for Dostoevsky freedom and groundlessness are even more sacred to him than the truths of Christianity that he also believed in. Freedom alone frees. Otherwise we are slaves to something within ourselves that teaches us endlessly and falsely that it is ourselves. This great book of Dostoevsky has many words and lines that imply that without freedom, a freedom that eliminates once and for all any enemy self, we are not ourselves as God created us. Yes, the words of Stavrogin that Shatov repeats with passion are "religious prating". But these words of Stavrogin that no longer have any meaning for him will allow Shatov to place out in the open the alien seed that is strangling his being and cut it out of his being once and for all by revealing the words came from a being as empty and as meaningless as himself without God. The genius of Dostoevsky will create the conversion of a man enslaved by an idea who frees himself not by means of holy and true words from a holy man like Saint Paul but by rooting out of his soul words that are empty and false coming from Stavrogin. The "religious prating" will lead Shatov to freedom and perhaps to God once he dares in the night to speak soul to soul and man to man to his soulless brother with his heart.

"I don't agree that you've not altered anything," Stavrogin observed cautiously. "You accepted them with ardour, and in your ardour have transformed them unconsciously. The very fact that you reduce God to a simple attribute of nationality..."

Right then something changes in Stavrogin. He is no longer indifferent as before. "He suddenly began watching Shatov with intense and peculiar attention, not so much his words as himself."

Shatov shouts at him, "I reduce God to the attribute of nationality? On the contrary, I raise the people to God." He continues in a long passionate analysis of how other nations, the Romans, the Greeks, the French related the nation to God. Then, with Stavrogin observing "not so much his words as himself", Shatov ends his long analysis by screaming madly, "Can you think me such a fool, Stavrogin, that I can't distinguish whether my words at this moment are the rotten old commonplaces that have been ground out in all the Slavophile mills in Moscow, or a perfectly new saying, the last word, the sole word of renewal and resurrection. and ... and what do I care for your laughter at this minute! What do I care if you utterly, utterly fail to understand me, not a word, not a sound! Oh, how I despise your haughty laughter and your look at this minute!"

But Shatov does care. He wants "the last word, the sole word of renewal and resurrection" but he is now driven mad because he realizes the more he seeks religious truth in Stavrogin, the more Stavrogin just reveals that he is so empty of such truth that his internal nothingness can only drive him more mad. "He jumped up from his seat; there was positively foam on his lips." Stavrogin, still with self-control, at least realizes that Shatov is deeply moved about the question of religious belief. They talk back and forth. When Shatov criticises him for speaking indirectly and jokingly about religion, he forces Stavrogin to come directly to the subject.

"Stavrogin looked coldly at him. 'I only wanted to know, do you believe in God, yourself?'

'I believe in Russia… I believe in her orthodoxy….I believe in the body of Christ...I believe that the new coming will take place in Russia...I believe...' Shatov muttered frantically."

Shatov is very close to *the secret treasure* that Sonya tried to help Raskolnikov reach by her patient sincere belief in Christ and God. But she failed. The Underground Man was almost led to love by the love of Lisa but he could not make a leap of faith from the nothingness within him to the love she offered him and instead treated her as a prostitute. Mr. Golyadkin could not believe in himself deeply enough to get rid forever of his double, of his false Mr. Golyadkin. And now we have the brave and good and passionate Shatov, the soul of Russia, just on the point of real belief because he has had the courage to face and drive out of his soul the false words of Stavrogin but…

"And in God?" asks Stavrogin, the false Christ, the false Tzar. "In God?"

"I...I will believe in God."

Shatov has probed far into himself by relentlessly pursuing inside Stavrogin his falsity and the falsity inside himself that Stavrogin planted in his being. But Shatov is only close to *the secret treasure*. Only freedom will take him there and no one can be really free who does not first reach the place in the heart where feeling and not reason announces to the self passionately that only the heart can free us by opening to us the freedom necessary to reach the love and grace of the world of God. Shatov *almost* believes but it is not enough. How can he find a way in the dead of night facing an empty soulless man to speak from his heart and only from his heart?

"Not one muscle moved in Stavrogin's face. Shatov looked passionately and defiantly at him, as though he would have scorched him with his eyes."

"'But who cares about me? We're discussing you not me. I'm nothing but a man without talent, and all I have to offer is my blood, like anyone else who has no talent. But the hell with my blood ... I'm concerned with you. I've been waiting for you here for two years and for the past hour I've felt I were dancing naked before you…'"

Stavrogin matters because he still seems to Shatov a leader, a man more powerful than himself, who can perhaps lead him where he needs to go and where he can not go by his own power. But then Stavrogin complains that "everyone seems so anxious to force some banner upon me". And when he complains that Pyotor Stepanovich is one of those who want him to raise a banner, he happens to say in passing that Pyotor noted that he had an "uncanny talent for crime". This all at once gives Shatov the chance to shift the talk from his own lack of belief in God to Stavrogin's sins. This path does lead Shatov to the depths of feeling in his heart for Stavrogin. It finally gets the two to the heart of their relationship and at the very instant when they might have joined, joined like two men who had reached together a holy place like the place where Sonya has her secret treasure, they split forever and go their separate ways each alone in the night.

"'Hm,' Shatov said with a fierce snort after the mention of Stavrogin's talent for crime. 'and is it true that in Petersburg you belonged to some secret society that practiced the most bestial sensuality? Is it true that you could give some tips to the Marquis de Sade himself? Is it true that you used to entice children and corrupt them? Speak up, man, and don't you dare lie to me,' he shouted, completely beside himself. 'Nikolai Stavrogin can not lie to Shatov, who hit him in the face! Tell me the whole truth, and if what I've said is true I'll kill you here and now!'

'I never harmed children,' Stavrogin said. But he said it after a silence that had lasted too long, He had turned pale and his eyes glowed.

Shatov went on imperiously, without taking his shining eyes from Stavrogin. 'Is it true that you said that you could see no distinction in beauty between some voluptuous, bestial prank and a heroic feat such as giving one's life for the good of mankind? Is it true that you found an equal beauty and an equal pleasure in those extremes?'"

"'It's impossible to answer just like that — — I won't answer,' muttered Stavrogin, who might well have got up and gone away, but who did not get up and go away.

'I don't know either why evil is hateful and good beautiful, but I know why the sense of that distinction is effaced and lost in people like Stavrogins,' Shatov persisted, trembling all over. 'Shall I tell you why you married that woman, so shamefully, so disgracefully? You did it precisely because the senselessness and the disgrace of it bordered on genius! Ah, you don't content yourself with teetering on the brink of the abyss — — you plunge into it headfirst. You married her to satisfy your passion for martyrdom, your passion for remorse; you went through with it for moral sensuality. It was a deliberate laceration of the nerves. You couldn't resist making such a challenge to common sense. Think of it — — Stavrogin and a wretched, half-witted, crippled beggar! By the way, did you feel a voluptuous thrill when you bit the governor's ear? Did you, you good-for-nothing loafing little snob?'

'You're a real psychologist,' Stavrogin said, turning paler and paler. 'though you're partly mistaken about my reasons for marrying. But who could possibly have supplied you with all that information?' he asked, smiling with an effort. 'Was it Kirillov? But he had nothing to do with it.'

'Why have you turned so pale?'

'But what is it you want?' Stavrogin asked, raising his voice at last. 'I've been taking a lashing from you for the last half hour. You might at least let me go civilly, unless you have good reason for treating me like this.'

' Good reason?'

'Certainly. The least you could do now is explain what you're after. I've been waiting for it, but so far I've seen nothing but mad spite on your part. So now, please, will you unlock the gate for me?'

'He stood up. Shatov rushed frantically towards him.

'Kiss the earth — — water it with your tears and ask for forgiveness!', he shouted, clutching Stavrogin by the shoulder."

'I didn't kill you, though, that morning…...I drew my hands back…..' Stavrogin said, looking down and appearing to be suffering great pain.

' Come on, spill the rest of it! You came to warn me of danger, you've allowed me to speak; tomorrow you will announce your marriage publically. Do you think I can't see from your face that some new, dreadful idea is now taking hold of you? Stavrogin, why am I condemned to believe in you through all eternity? Do you think I could ever speak like this to anyone else? I'm usually very restrained, but I haven't hesitated to bare my soul before you, nor was I afraid to caricature the great idea by putting it into words, since it was Stavrogin who was listening to me. As though I'd be able to prevent myself from kissing the spots where your feet have walked when you leave here...I can't tear you out of my heart, Nikolai Stavrogin!'

'I'm sorry I can't love you in return, Shatov,' Stavrogin said cooly."

The heart has entered the conversation and with it, at least in Shatov, love. But no love passes between the two men. No grace from God enters either man's soul but Shatov's soul is now free of Stavrogin's influence. A false Christ has converted a disciple by freeing him from his devilish influence. The freedom Shatov discovers in his soul may send him on a path to God.

16

Ivan Karamazov, one of the three brothers in Dostoevsky's last novel *The Brothers Karamazov*, creates the Grand Inquisitor scene. This world-famous scene has been correctly praised for adding a radical new dimension to traditional Christian beliefs.

The core of this new dimension is Dostoevsky's belief in the religious necessity of freedom. To express his doctrine of religious freedom he creates a dramatic confrontation of two beings outside of normal time and normal circumstances with definite resemblances to the scene between Stavrogin and Shatov. It is not a scene in the novel but a scene created by a character in the novel, Ivan Karamazov. He has imagined and written the scene and he reveals its contents to his brother, Alyosha Karamazov, at a meeting between them in a restaurant. A central idea expressed both in the dialogue between Shatov and Stavrogin and expressed by a Cardinal of the Catholic Church, the Grand Inquisitor, in Ivan Karamazov's scene is that Roman Catholicism is no longer Christian because it yielded to the temptation to establish the church as an earthly kingdom. Shatov says to Stavrogin, "...you went further: you believed that Roman Catholicism was not Christianity; you asserted that Rome proclaimed Christ subject to the third temptation of the devil. Announcing to all the world that Christ without an earthly kingdom cannot hold his ground upon earth, Catholicism by so doing proclaimed Antichrist and ruined the whole Western world." The ninety-year-old Cardinal of the Roman Catholic Church expresses the same idea to Christ who listens to him behind prison bars in Ivan Karamazov's imagined Grand Inquisitor scene. The old Cardinal says, "We are not working with Thee, but with him — that is our mystery. It's long — eight centuries — since we have been on his side and not on Thine. Just eight centuries ago, we took from him what Thou didst reject with scorn, that last gift he offered Thee, showing you all the kingdoms of the earth. We took from him Rome and the sword of Caesar, and proclaimed ourselves sole rulers of the earth...We have taken the sword of Caesar, and in taking it, of course, have rejected Thee and followed him."

Ivan Karamazov is a good and passionate man like Shatov who has like Shatov a tortured soul that can not arrive at a truth that can satisfy it. He is an atheist principally because he cannot accept that a God could exist and yet allow innocent children to suffer. In his Grand Inquisitor scene, we do not have a false Christ, a

Stavrogin, who produces a non-christian conversion in a Shatov. But we do have again a new creation of a Christ by Dostoevsky. Ivan Karamazov imagines for his scene the real Christ returned to earth and questioned by a Cardinal of the Catholic Church. And we do have another failed Christian conversion because the old Cardinal can not be converted to a true version of the Christian faith even standing directly before a real Christ in person.

17

The Christ in Ivan's imagined scene is locked up in a jail in Spain in the 15th century during the time of the Spanish Inquisition. He has returned to earth but the Spanish religious authorities conducting the Inquisition want nothing to do with him. They put him in jail. A very old man, the Grand Inquisitor, a Cardinal of the Catholic church, stands before the bars of Christ's jail cell and questions him. Christ never answers his questions but Dostoevsky brings out by means of them his own belief in the religious *necessity* of freedom. The old Cardinal accuses Christ of giving the divine gift of freedom to man and argues passionately that man is too weak to accept the gift. The Cardinal succeeds in expressing directly and explicitly Dostoevsky's belief in freedom and makes us believe that freedom is a divine gift from God without which there can be no true relationship between man and God.

The Grand Inquisitor poem by Ivan Karamazov also teaches us that knowledge, our human knowledge based on logical processes in our mind, has nothing to do with God. Our knowledge, which the Bible says caused the fall of Adam and Eve, is incapable of being applied to God to receive from him some idea of his existence except some false idea of it that fits with the rational thoughts of our mind. God will not receive and answer questions put to him formed by human knowledge just as the silent Christ behind bars will not answer the piercing and profound questions about the Christian religion put to him by the old Cardinal in the Grand Inquisitor scene. The Cardinal is forced by Christ's silence to answer for him and his deep and tragic pessimistic thoughts about Christianity do make him speak Dostoevsky's truth, a truth that the old Cardinal is against with his whole heart and soul, the truth that God's only answer to our questions about his nature is that we give up our reliance on rational knowledge and find our true nature and God's nature by relying on freedom. The religious ideas and religious practices that the old Cardinal has forced members of his church to accept in order to deprive them of a God-given freedom are mortal dangers for our souls and, whether we are believers or not, only freedom bravely used against them can save us.

The freedom Dostoevsky reveals in the scene is the freedom that God creates along with grace and as a vital path to grace. It is not simply human freedom to do whatever a person wants. It is a freedom that is reached by a mysterious and brave free jump into some unknown area of our being that reveals by the discovery of a new dimension of ourselves how profoundly necessary is freedom to our human nature. God gives grace freely and grace is itself, so to speak, the divine substance of freedom. Christ as revealed by the three temptations of the devil in the gospel is full of God's grace but the very condition of this grace is that it must be given freely and so with grace from God Christ is also free to abandon God and grace and yield to temptation. This freedom that comes with grace is Dostoevsky's *necessary* religious freedom. Grace that is truly grace must freely face and reject a temptation that can possibly eliminate the presence of grace. Christ was full of his father's grace and free to reject it and yield to temptation. But the power of grace which is also the power of God's love gave him enough strength to resist temptation. Dostoevsky tells us in the Grand Inquisitor scene that God grants us this freedom even before and without any experience of grace. If we have the power within us to reach this freedom then we do experience the near presence of grace for the freedom gives us a deep sense that we have found at last a mysterious path to our true self. It is in fact this moment of pure freedom that a person about to be born again spiritually must reach by a leap of faith into the unknown when he gives up his normal self-created self and calls out to God for his divine help. But we must understand that this freedom of Dostoevsky is experienced both before and also after the experience of grace. A true Christian does not experience grace just once. He is always seeking a union or reunion with God's grace by using his God-given *religious* freedom to guide him away from every type of temptation offered to entice his being from the union of his will with the will of God. This means that a behavior guided by some sort of rational moral standard is the victim of a process that is of no help in reaching God's grace and love and in maintaining union with them. And, just as important, when grace is experienced it is the death of grace to rely exclusively on some rational moral standard to do good. We must be good and only do good because goodness gives our freedom a vital and substantial presence in our heart of divine love but in our human condition, as Christ experienced it on earth, temptations never cease to tempt our souls and we must be brave enough to face them in a state of complete freedom and reject them in the name of God's grace which a divine knowledge tells us will surely come to our aid as it came to Christ's aid. Dostoevsky's freedom is absolutely necessary both to receive grace for the first time and also to live a good and moral life relying on continual infusions into the soul of God's grace as the result of living with a freedom created by God.

In describing how Christ freely faced one of the three temptations of the devil, the old Inquisitor describes Dostoevsky's freedom concretely with unmistakable words. His freedom comes to men according to the old Cardinal "at the great moments of their life, the moments of their deepest, most agonizing spiritual difficulties". At these moments men reach a state of divine freedom when they dare to reject everything they are and everything they know and "cling only to the free verdict of the heart". The Cardinal of the Catholic church tells the silent Christ on the other side of the cell's bars, "When the wise and dread spirit set Thee on the pinnacle of the Temple and said to Thee, 'if Thou wouldst know whether Thou art the Son of God then cast Thyself down for it is written: the angels shall hold him up lest he fall and bruise himself, and Thou shalt know then whether Thou art the Son of God and shalt prove then how great is Thy faith in Thy Father'. But Thou didst refuse and would not cast Thyself down. Oh, of course, Thou didst proudly and well like God; but the weak, unruly race of men, are they Gods? Oh, Thou didst know then that in taking one step, in making one movement to cast Thyself down, Thou wouldst be tempting God and have lost all Thy faith in Him, and would have been dashed to pieces against that earth which Thou didst come to save. And the wise spirit that tempted Thee would have rejoiced. But I ask again, are there many like Thee? And couldst Thou believe for one moment that men, too, could face such a temptation? Is the nature of men such that they can reject miracle, and at the great moments of their life, the moments of their deepest, most agonizing spiritual difficulties, cling only to the free verdict of the heart?"

Shatov at the moment of his "deepest, most agonizing spiritual difficulties" freely clung "only to the free verdict of the heart" and discovered there love. One possible outcome from Dostoevsky's freedom is love. "Thou didst crave faith given freely not based on miracle," says the Inquisitor. "Thou didst crave for free love and not the base raptures of the slave…" But the enemy of the freedom that can lead to the verdict of the heart is the verdict of the mind. The Inquisitor accuses Christ saying that "instead of giving a firm foundation for setting the conscience of man at rest for ever, Thou didst choose all that is exceptional,vague and enigmatic". "Thou didst desire man's free love, that he should follow Thee freely…Man must hereafter with free heart decide for himself what is good and what is evil…" "Nothing is more seductive for man than his freedom of conscience, but nothing is a greater cause of suffering." The old Cardinal is against free love, against a free belief in Christ not based on miracles, against a free heart, against "all that is exceptional, vague and enigmatic". He is for whatever makes man content and happy by enslaving his mind to prevent it from using his God-given freedom to open itself to the world of free belief and free love which is discovered not using the mind but the heart.

18

Men and women who are free can be penetrated and changed spiritually by a holy spirit suddenly born in their souls. This is the main theme of *The Brothers Karamazov.* This holy spirit reaches into the souls of three characters in the novel through the Christ-like love that Alyosha Karamazov expresses to them personally, Dimitri Karamazov, Grushenka, the woman he loves, and a young man of fourteen, Kolya.

At the beginning of the novel, Dostoevsky describes for us the remarkable character of Alyosha Karamazov. He is presented to us not as holy and religious but as so extraordinarily free of the ordinary desires of a young man that he seems holy. It becomes clear as we learn more about him and observe his actions that Dostoevsky personalizes the Holy Spirit in his character. Throughout the novel Alyosha in scene after scene embodies the Holy Spirit and influences others to communicate with himself and with others through love. Dostoevsky reveals Alyosha's extraordinary capacity for inspiring love in his introductory remarks about his character at the very beginning of the novel, "...the gift of making himself loved directly and unconsciously was inherent in him, in his very nature, so to speak". In particular, he tries to infuse his spirit of love, his holy spirit into the personhood of his brothers. Sonya haunts Raskolnikov with her sacred love, her secret treasure. Liza haunts the Underground Man with a love that seems impossible to have ever arisen in her. The prince in the *Idiot* haunts the people he meets in Petersburg with Christian goodness. And now Alyosha haunts his brothers and others with a goodness that does not come from himself, that comes from the spirit of God within him. He is a walking, breathing, talking representation throughout the novel of the Holy Spirit. Dostoevsky by inventing this device artistically, by emphasizing Alyosha's exceptional nature, infuses a presence of grace into this his last and most religious novel. Alyosha loves his brothers Dimitri and Ivan and as the plot develops he succeeds in making both of them confess in turn that they love him. The theme of possible love between three men, between Kirillov, Shatov, and Stavrogin, was implicit in *The Possessed* but was expressed openly only by Shatov. In *The Brothers Karamazov* the love is realized and confessed openly. And then after a long dramatic sequence of events, mysteriously, in a sequence that expresses a religious teaching of equal importance with the revelation of religious freedom in the Grand Inquisitor scene, the religious genius of Dostoevsky reaches its fulfillment by creating before our eyes the transfer of grace and love from the holy monk Zossima to Alyosha, from Alyosha to Grushenka and then from Grushenka in turn to Dimitri Karamazov. She and he find together their human relationship supported mysteriously because of Alyosha's influence by a Christ-like love. A holy spirit enters their souls and unites them forever even though their relationship before was not holy at all.

The elder Zossima, a holy man living in a monastery, is the source of this holy spirit. It is by love of the man Zossima that Alyosha was himself transformed from merely a young man free and aloof from the normal temptations of youth to a religious believer. He has entered the local monastery and lives as a monk under the guidance of Zossima. Dostoevsky explains that Alyosha's goal is "to attain perfect freedom, that is, from self; to escape the lot of those who have lived their whole life without finding their true selves in themselves." But Dostoevsky's goal is not to merely express the Holy Spirit by the saintly words of Zossima or by creating a holy spirit in Alyosha as merely some literary symbol of the Holy Spirit. No, he will show us the Holy Spirit actually at work concretely transforming human souls. He says of Alyosha in his first description of him that his elder Zosima stood "as a solitary example before him". But Alyosha with his extraordinary capacity for making himself loved is not worried by Zossima's solitary spiritual qualities. He says of him, "'No matter. He is holy. He carries in his heart the secret of renewal for all: that power which will, at last, establish truth on the earth, and all men will be holy and love one another, and there will be no more rich nor poor, no exalted nor humbled, but all will be as the children of God, and the true Kingdom of Christ will come.' That was the dream in Alyosha's heart." But an example and a dream in his heart is not enough. As the drama develops, the Holy Spirit must actually transform his soul by a profound second conversion that fills his soul with a religious joy that he did not know previously. And he must also, if the Holy Spirit is truly within him, transfer this divine presence of God that lives eternally among humans to other humans.

19

Dostoevsky's demands that we face the "verdict of the heart" to reach freedom. It can lead to a liberating divine love. For him human history is not governed, as it appears, exclusively by fate. The son of God himself has instituted the Holy Spirit on earth and no power on earth will ever be strong enough to remove it. But freedom discovered by the "verdict of the heart" can also lead to enigma and despair. He reveals this possible negative outcome from freedom by describing a scene in which a Karamazov brother, Dimitri, is suffering a deep and agonizing emotional pain. Dimitri is not only passionately in love with Grushenka, he is also totally enslaved by his love. Grushenka is someone willing to sell her beauty for money. She was seduced and then abandoned by a man at eighteen and has been in a business relationship for five years with a wealthy old merchant now near death. She plays the tease with Dimitri Karamazov who is madly in love with her. He is a totally free spirit who is willing to do anything, including perhaps murdering his own father, to prevent any other man from winning her. She is seriously considering selling herself for money by giving herself to Dimitri's father, Fyodor Karamazov, who has promised her 3000 roubles if she comes to his house and makes love with him. She is also thinking of perhaps marrying him legally because he is a rich man. The idea that later in the key scene of the novel she could be transformed in her soul by a holy spirit communicated to her personally by Alyosha seems thoroughly beyond the possible.

Alyosha leaves his monastery to return to his father's house by a shortcut through the back streets of the town and discovers his step-brother Dimitri waiting in a garden near Grushenka's house in case she comes out to go to his father who is waiting for her in a state of lustful excitement. Alyosha joins his brother in the garden and the two talk. Dimitri's love for Grushenka is nothing like the Christ-like love in the spirit of his brother Alyosha. Dimitri says to him, " ...being in love doesn't mean loving. You may be in love with a woman and yet hate her." The love he feels for his brother, an angel, a holy spirit, is the opposite type of love, the love that ascends to God and does not descend like Dimitri's love for Grushenka. But even though he is falling into a pit, the love for God is still mixed with the love for Grushenka that causes his fall "...for when I do leap into the pit, I go headlong with my heels up, and am pleased to be falling in that degrading attitude, and pride myself upon it. And in the very depths of that degradation I begin a hymn of praise. Let me be accursed. Let me be vile and base, only let me kiss the hem of the veil in which my God is shrouded. Though I may be following the devil, I am Thy son, O Lord, and I love Thee, and I feel the joy without which the world can not stand." His fall is one of the most moving passages in Dostoevsky. We feel the terrible despair that can grip the free man who has thrown away reason and knowledge and accepted "the verdict of the heart". He can not find answers anymore. There are no answers and the questions of a truly free man like Dimitri are loaded with the terrible burden of mystery which most of us humans, as the old Grand Inquisitor warned, are too weak to bear. Dimitri says with deep feeling to his angelic brother Alyosha, "...sensual love is a tempest — worse than a tempest! Beauty is a terrible and awesome thing! It is terrible because it has not been fathomed and never can be fathomed, for God sets us nothing but riddles. Here the boundaries meet and all contradictions meet side by side. I am not a cultivated man, brother, but I've thought a lot about this. It's terrible what mysteries there are! Too many riddles weigh men down on earth....Beauty! I can't endure the thought that a man of lofty mind and heart begins with the ideal of the Madonna and ends with the ideal of Sodom. What's still more awful is that a man with the ideal of Sodom in his soul does not renounce the ideal of the Madonna and his heart may be on fire with that ideal, genuinely on fire, just as in his days of youth and innocence....The awful thing is that beauty is mysterious as well as terrible. God and the devil are fighting there and the battlefield is the heart of man."

In another scene, when Ivan Karamazov meets with his brother Alyosha in a restaurant, we also feel in their conversation that "the battlefield is the heart of man".

Ivan expresses his view that it is impossible to love one's neighbor. He says to Alyosha, "I could never understand how one can love one's neighbors. It's just one's neighbors, to my mind, that one can't love." Alyosha answers that "an almost Christ-like love" nonetheless exists. He says, "There's a great deal of love in mankind, an almost Christ-like love. I know that myself, Ivan." Ivan admits that children are lovable but not adults. He tells Alyosha the story of an innocent child who is tortured by adults but still prays to "dear, kind God". "Why the whole world of knowledge is not worth that child's prayer to 'dear, kind god'. I say nothing of the sufferings of grown-up people." Shortly after he says, "I understand nothing. I don't want to understand anything now. I want to stick to the fact. I made up my mind long ago not to understand. If I try to understand anything, I shall be false to the fact and I have determined to stick to the fact." Ivan has explained in a long tirade that whether one understands or not, whether one believes or not, one should love life. "Do you understand anything of my tirade, Alyosha?" Alyosha says, "I think everyone should love life above everything in the world." "Love life more than the meaning of it?" "Certainly, love it, regardless of all logic as you say, it must be regardless of logic, and only then one will understand the meaning of it." Ivan is about to recite to Alyosha his story of Christ and the Grand Inquisitor. In it the old Cardinal will use knowledge and logic and understanding as weapons to reject Christ. Ivan has already said in the restaurant to his brother both that he loves him and that he accepts that there is a God but that he believes like his Grand Inquisitor that it is impossible to understand God. "I can't expect to understand about God." God's purpose Ivan says "is utterly beyond our ken". Ivan in his story of the Grand Inquisitor allows his old Cardinal to try to crush Christ with rational knowledge even though he himself is for "stupidity". He tells Alyosha, "The stupider one is the closer one is to reality." "Intelligence is a knave but stupidity is honest and straight-forward."

20

The central goal of this long and complex novel is to crucify an innocent man, Dimitri Karamazov, by putting him in jail for a murder he did not commit. The hammer that nails him to his cross is rationality, the same rationality that Raskolikov tried to conquer by carrying it to an atrocious extreme, the rationality that the Underground Man despises as two-plus-two-makes-four. It is truly amazing that Dostoevsky in one novel sends his hero, Raskolnikov, to jail because of the evil way he employs rationality and in another novel sends to jail a hero whose free and bold actions on the day of his father's murder convict him of the crime because police officials can arrive at no other conclusion but his guilt employing for their judgement rationality.

It is also truly amazing that side by side with the regular workings of rational knowledge with its deadly indifference to real life, we have also as a central unfolding in the novel the expression of a condition in life that the holy elder Zossima speaks about on the day of his death. Speaking of his fascination with tales in the Bible where the devil and God compete for the souls of men, he says, "But the greatness of it lies just in the fact that it is a mystery — that the passing earthly show and the eternal verity are brought together in it. In the face of the earthly truth, the eternal truth is accomplished."

Let us state exactly the "eternal truth" Dostoevsky accomplishes in the drama "in the face of the earthly truth". The holy spirit of divine love passes from the soul of the elder Zossima to the soul of Alyosha uniting them. Then the same spirit passes from Alyosha into the soul of Grushenka, changing her radically and mysteriously even though it happens so subtly that she herself at first is not aware of the full extent of the change within her. Then this holy love from Alyosha that is now also in Grushenka in turn passes from her to Dimitri.

But outwardly, as the internal drama of holy intercommunion rolls on, the "earthly truth" is also accomplishing itself. Dimitri, a free man, a man who has thrown away all thought of confining himself to rational conduct because of his love for Grushenka, accomplishes his own doom by inadvertently and unknowingly laying down concrete evidence step by step that proves to authorities that he murdered his father. Raskolnikov murders two women with an axe guided by rationality yet despite this "earthly truth", a divinely inspired young woman, whose "earthly truth" is that she is a prostitute, unites her life with his. Dimitri has murdered no one but the free and unthinking actions he takes in pursuit of his love Grushenka condemn him like Raskolnikov to prison and like Raskolnikov he also unites eternally with a young woman changed like Sonya by a divine love operating within her.

The elder Zossima, on the day of his death, gives us on his death bed talking to his fellow monks the theological basis for the conversion his disciple Alyosha produces in Grushenka. He speaks profoundly about the main theme of the novel, the holy brotherly relationships that are possible among humans. He says, "... in truth we are each responsible to all for all, it's only that men don't know this. If they knew it, the world would be a paradise at once." "Look around you," he says shortly afterwards, "at the gifts of God, the clear sky, the pure air, the tender grass, the birds, nature is beautiful and sinless, and we, only we, are sinful and foolish, and we don't understand that life is heaven, for we have only to understand that and it will be at once fulfilled in all its beauty, we shall embrace each other and weep." "Heaven," he went on, "lies hidden within all of us — here it lies hidden in me now, and if it will, it will be revealed to me tomorrow and for all time." "Until you become really, in actual fact, a brother to everyone, brotherhood will not come to pass." We will see that Alyosha will love Grushenka as a brother because she in turn has had pity on him since he suffers because so many people, believers and unbelievers, have expressed hatred and jealousy towards his dead sacred elder. But meanwhile the elder still living but lying on his deathbed explains how destructive individuality is the problem. "For everyone strives to keep his individuality as apart as possible, wishes to secure the greatest possible fullness of life for himself; but meantime all his efforts result not in attaining fullness of life but self-destruction, for instead of self-realization he ends by arriving at complete solitude. All mankind in our age have split into units, they all keep apart, each in his own groove; each one holds aloof, hides himself and hides what he has, from the rest, and he ends by being repelled by others and repelling them." But some monks like himself and Alyosha keep the truth of Christ alive in Russia. "The monastic way is very different. Obedience, fasting and prayer are laughed at, yet through them lies the way to real, true freedom. I cut off my superfluous and unnecessary desires, I subdue my proud and wonton will and chastise it with obedience, and with God's help I attain freedom of spirit and with it spiritual joy." His love as he talks is boundless, "Brothers, have no fear of men's sin. Love a man even in his sin, for that is the semblance of divine love and is the highest love on earth. Love all God's creation, the whole and every grain of sand in it. Love every leaf, every ray of God's light. Love the animals, love the plants, love everything. If you love everything, you will perceive the divine mystery in things." No one expects hearing such boundless talk of the need for divine love that the elder will die the same day.

Alyosha sheds tears at the passing of his elder. The holy man has left him behind on earth with the mission to spread about in the hearts of men the holy spirit of brotherly love. But the general hostile reaction to what happens after the elder's death causes a great change to take place within him. Excited crowds gathered near the monastery expecting a miracle. Both believers and non-believers waited impatiently for something to happen and some even began resenting that the expected miracle was so late in coming. Then the hope for a miracle was destroyed when "an odour of corruption began to come from the coffin, growing more and more perceptible, and by three o'clock in the afternoon it could no longer be mistaken and was, indeed, becoming gradually stronger and stronger." Everyone remembered other monks and priests who had died and whose bodies were buried without showing any signs of decomposition. The great majority of people in the surrounding area including some monks and priests turn hatefully against the dead Zossima. The general reaction is that there will be no miracle because the odour from the body of Zossima means that he was not in reality a holy man. Dostoevsky then takes great pains to explain that this had a powerful influence on the heart and soul of Alyosha "forming a crisis and a turning-point in his spiritual life, causing a violent shock…". But the shock does not result from Alyosha's disappointment that there will be no miracle. It results from the fierce negativity and even hatred expressed by the general public towards the holy man he loved because communication with him had lit up his soul with divine, Christ-like love.

Dostoevsky writes that Alyosha loves passionately and can not respond to the death lukewarmly as perhaps other youths might respond. Indeed he writes, " It really is much more admirable to give way to an emotion, however unreasonable, which springs from a great love, than not to give way to it at all. And that is all the more so when one is young, for a youth who is invariably reasonable does not inspire much confidence and isn't worth much…" And as an enemy of rationality because it is the tool that aids "the passing earthly show" and out of love for his hero who represents "the eternal verity", he writes, "I am glad my young hero did not turn out to be so reasonable at such a moment, for a man who is not a fool will have enough time to see reason, but if there is no love in a young man's heart at such an exceptional moment, then when will it come?" The faith in Alyosha's soul is not broken but the human side of his soul is shocked. His heart is bleeding because he needed not miracles as a result of the death "but only 'higher justice', which, according to his belief, had been violated, and it was this that dealt such a sudden and cruel blow to his heart." "And now the man who, according to his expectations, ought to have been raised above everyone else in the whole world, that very man, instead of receiving the glory that was his due was suddenly cast down and disgraced!" "He could not bear without mortification, without bitterness even, that the most righteous of the righteous should have been exposed to such jeering and spiteful mockery of a crowd so thoughtless and so inferior to him." "Where was Providence and its finger? Why did it hide its finger at the most critical moment (thought Alyosha) and seem to be anxious itself to submit to the blind. dumb, pitiless laws of nature?" Alyosha's heart for these reasons was bleeding. He feels so bitter that he can not remain in the monastery and leaves without remaining with his fellow monks for the services going on for the dead man. He himself loses awareness that the holy spirit, "the heaven" that his elder said "lies hidden within all of us", is within him still. Alyosha walks away from the monastery and in his bitterness seems to be now on the side of "earthly truth". He walks aimlessly in a field and lies under a tree motionless with his face downwards to the ground. Little indicates that along with the "earthly truth" the "eternal truth" will be soon be accomplished at the house of Grushenka, a free, worldly, beautiful young woman who lives comfortably and independently because of a five-year relationship with an old merchant after having previously been seduced at eighteen and abandoned by the man who seduced her. The finger of Providence is not absent. It is waiting ready to act at Grushenka's house.

21

Dostoevsky's final and supreme message to us is that salvation is possible in an evil world but knowledge of God is not possible. Our human knowledge constructed by rational processes in our mind does not apply to God. Men must live like Dimitri Karamazov with their mind and heart open and free and fearlessly face "enigma". Since rational knowledge does not relate to God and enslaves man, man must first and foremost seek freedom. Life should not be a continuous search guided by reason for whatever is to our advantage. As Ivan says about life to his brother Alyosha in his conversation with him in the restaurant, "It's not a matter of intellect or logic, it's loving with one's inside, with one's stomach." In conversation with a young man named Kolya, Alyosha goes so far as to praise being ridiculous , "...what does ridiculous mean? Does it matter how many times a man is or seems to be ridiculous? Besides, today almost all people of ability are terribly afraid of making themselves ridiculous and that makes them unhappy." For our knowledge, only what is sensible and reasonable counts and what is ridiculous is absurd because it cannot lead to something that is to our advantage. Rational knowledge degrades humans and judges the free movements of the spirit in our soul ridiculous. So love among men, rare as it is, is the only positive truth Dostoevsky has for us because it is a path to salvation as well as to freedom from evil and knowledge. For Dostoevsky, the "earthly truth" lives proudly and abundantly in countless forms of human life that all appear justified because they are based on rationality and are advantageous. But the "eternal truth" is love because its foundation is the Holy Spirit that no human form of life can ever kill because it was instituted on earth by the sacrifice of the Son of God on a cross.

Rakitin, a young man of Alyosha's age, comes across him lying on the ground. He lives also at the monastery and pretends to be devout and religious. Alyosha knows that he is not a true Christian. Dostoevsky writes about him, "He was particularly clever in getting around people and assuming whatever part he thought most to their taste, if he detected the slightest advantage to himself from doing so." He is an inveterate rationalist out to take advantage of every opportunity for advancement to some higher social position. Alyosha shouts at him angrily to leave him alone. Rakitin senses he has changed, even that like himself he perhaps now no longer believes. "Damn it all", says Rakitin, "a thirteen-year-old schoolboy doesn't believe in that now....So you're angry with your God now are you?" "I haven't taken up arms against God," says Alyosha with a wry smile because he knows he can not make an unbeliever understand his condition. "I simply don't accept his world." ""You don't accept his world? What do you mean?' Rakitin asked, thinking over his answer for a moment. 'What rot is this?' "

Alyosha does not answer and Rakitin, a thoroughly practical young man, switches the conversation to a practical matter. He asks his friend if he has had anything to eat. He offers him some sausage and when Alyosha accepts it he senses that he has perhaps changed. He offers to take Alyosha to his place to drink some vodka. He is amazed that Alyosha also accepts to do this. This change that he correctly observes acting in Alyosha is something that does not exist in himself. It is simply freedom. Alyosha has been shocked by the injustice of the hatred that most people have expressed for his beloved elder and he has taken a jump in his soul, however ridiculous it may seem, to freedom. If the real and practical world of humans is limited and practical like the world of Rakitin, if the men and women around him can not understand how divinely unjust is all hatred among them, if the possibility of divine love among themselves appears to them in their rational insanity absurd and ridiculous, then a man who has an unshakable faith in God will make the jump in his soul to freedom, if that is the only weapon possible against the injustice of human hearts enslaved by hatred. As the two young men walk towards Rakatin's place to drink vodka, he suggests to Alyosha that they go instead to Grushenka's house and visit her. Alyosha agrees to visit her.

The beautiful young woman is in a state of mind now like Alyosha's. She has lived well-off for five years in a relationship with an old merchant who is now near death. The man who seduced and abandoned her five years ago has returned seeking a new relationship with her. She is so inspired by the sudden possibility of a complete change in her life that she has made a jump in her soul like Alyosha. The new possibility demands on her part that she be free and that she act freely open now to all possibilities. She is actually waiting as the two young men walk to her house for a letter from her former lover asking her to travel in the carriage he has sent her to a nearby town to meet with him. She doesn't know what she will do. She is not thinking calmly and rationally as would Rakitin about using the new possibility only for her practical advantage. Her soul is on fire. She is free. Alyosha is free. Rakitin is so enslaved by his continuous search for whatever is to his advantage that he will be a third person present during words and actions between Alyosha and Grushenka and he will not understand even slightly the miracle of divine love that passes between the two. It fatally converts their hearts and souls to a new divine-human way of life that seems impossible to most men and women.

When the young men meet with Grushenka in her living room, Rakitin wants to know why she is dressed so well. She tells him she is expecting some good news "so that I can certainly do without poor Mitya now" and

"When it comes, I'll be off in a jiffy and you'll see no more of me. That's why I'm dressed up. To be ready." She feels she is done with "Mitya", Dimitri Karamazov. She was frightened when she heard the two young men at her door thinking for a few moments it might be Mitya. She thought it was Mitya trying to get in. She says that this afternoon she deceived him, that she told him a lie about her whereabouts. She says Mitya believes she is not at home when in reality, "I've been sitting locked in here, expecting a message". This beautiful young woman is preparing to fly off in a carriage to a new life with her former lover. She has done everything possible to keep Mitya away. She is frightened by him and done with him and yet just a few hours later that night in a hotel in another town she will make it clear to Mitya that love now joins her to him eternally and that she will never leave him. This miracle takes place in her heart because previously in the day love enters her heart from the holy spirit in the heart of Alyosha. In other words, something takes place miraculously in her that is outwardly ridiculous, irrational and unbelievable. But Grushenka tells Mitya later that day, "You know, Mitya, I think I'll enter a convent. Yes, I really shall some day. Alyosha said something to me today that I shall remember all my life." Alyosha says it to her. Rakitin hears what he says and it means nothing to him religiously. The Holy Spirit is for him ridiculous, irrational and unbelievable. As he listens to Alyosha in Grushenka's presence and watches him closely, it seems to him that Alyosha expresses no more than an irreligious normal sexual interest in a beautiful and seductive young woman. What takes place between Alyosha and Grushenka does not mean anything unusual or miraculous to him even though it is powerful enough to make the same seductive young woman confess the same day to Mitya, the man she has been trying to get rid of and is now eternally joined to, that she may one day enter a convent!

Grushenka tells Alyosha that she is so glad to see him. Later in the scene we find out that she promised Rakitin twenty-five roubles if he brought Alyosha to her. She tries to explain to Alyosha why she is glad to see him, "Why I'm so glad to see you, Alyosha, I'm sure I don't know. If you asked me, I couldn't tell you." "Don't you really know why you're so glad," asked Rakitin with a grin. "Why did you pester me to bring him before? You had some reason for it, hadn't you?" We can believe what Rakitin suggests, that her original reason was frivolous and seductive. But she claims, "I had quite a different reason before, but now that's over and done with. It's quite a different occasion." It is at this point different because her heart is now concentrating on a new possible relationship with a man who abandoned her five years previously.

She orders champagne and then notices that Alyosha is sad. Rakitin explains that Alyosha is sad because "His elder stank the place up". This makes Grushenka angry at Rakitin. She calls him a fool, asls Alyosha if she can sit on his knee and then springs up laughing and jumps on his knee "flinging her right arm caressingly around his neck". She says to him that if it makes him angry, she will get off. Alyosha is silent. Dostoevsky writes, "He did not answer just as though benumbed. But he did not feel what a man like Rakitin, for instance, who was watching him lasciviously from his corner, might have expected or imagined him to feel." A seduction is about to take place, but our rational knowledge will not allow us to believe that the Holy Spirit is the seducer.

As they wait for the champagne, Rakitin questions Grushenka about why she is so excited. She admits that her officer, her former lover, is near, that he is at a nearby town, that he is sending a messenger from there who will be at her house at any minute with a carriage to take her to him. Rakitin asks if Mitya knows about the officer. Grushenka answers that of course he doesn't know, that if he knew he would kill her. But she says that she is not afraid of him now and, still sitting on Alyosha's knee, she tries to make him smile. "Darling Alyosha, I'm looking at him now. Come on, smile at me, darling. Cheer up. Smile at my foolishness." Alyosha smiles and after Rakitin makes a comment suggesting Alyosha, a young man of little importance, is nonetheless making progress with her, she says to him, "You see, I love him with all my soul. I do, indeed! Alyosha, do you believe I love you with all my soul?" "The shameless hussy!" says Rakitin. "She's making a declaration of love, Alyosha!" "What about it? I do love him," says Grushenka. "And what about your officer? And the good news...?" asks Rakitin. "That has nothing to do with it." "Just like a woman," says Rakitin. "Don't make me angry, Rakitin," Grushenka cried warmly. "It has nothing to do with it. I love Alyosha in a different way. It's quite true, Alyosha. I had designs on you. I'm a low, violent creature, but there are times, Alyosha, when I look on you as my conscience. I go on thinking how a man like you must despise a bad woman like me..."

When the champagne comes, Alyosha has a sip and then decides not to drink any more. Grushenka says she will not drink any more either and tells Rakitin he can drink the whole bottle.

"What touching sentimentality," said Rakitin tauntingly, "and she's sitting on his knee, too! He's got something to grieve over, but what's the matter with you? He is rebelling against God and ready to eat sausage…"

"How so?"

"His elder died today, Father Zossima, the saint."

"'So Father Zossima is dead,' cried Grushenka. 'Good God, I did not know!' She crossed herself devoutly. 'Goodness, what have I been doing sitting on his knee like this at such a moment!' She started up as though in dismay, instantly slipped off his knee and sat down on the sofa.

Alyosha bent a long wondering look upon her and a light seemed to dawn in his face.

'Rakitin,' he said suddenly in a firm and loud voice, 'don't taunt me with having rebelled against God. I don't want to feel angry with you, so you must be kinder too. I've lost a treasure such as you have never had, and you cannot judge me now. You had much better look at her — do you see how she has pity on me? I came here to find a wicked soul — I felt drawn to evil because I was base and evil myself, and I've found a true sister, I have found a treasure — a loving heart. She had pity on me just now…Agrafena Alexandrovna, I'm speaking of you. You've raised my soul from the depths.'

Alyosha's lips were quivering and he caught his breath.

'She has saved you, it seems,' laughed Rakitin spitefully. 'And she meant to get you in her clutches, do you realize that?'

'Stay Rakitin.' Grushenka jumped up. 'Hush, both of you. Now I'll tell you about it. Hush, Alyosha, your words made me ashamed, for I am bad and not good — that's what I am. And you hush, Rakitin, because you are telling lies. I had the low idea of trying to get him in my clutches, but now you are lying, now it's all different. And don't let me hear anything more from you, Rakitin.'

All this Grushenka said with extreme emotion.

'They are both crazy,' said Rakitin, looking at them with amazement. 'I feel as though I were in a madhouse. They're both getting so feeble they'll begin crying in a minute.'

'I shall begin to cry. I shall,' repeated Grushenka. 'He called me his sister and I shall never forget that…'"

Rakitin does not get what is happening within them. It has nothing to do with the settled and firm state normally within us that reassures our consciousness that rational awareness backed up by our human knowledge constitutes the true foundation that makes us who we are. But the change within Alyosha and Grushenka is subtle. A holy spirit is passing between them that does not come from themselves. Dostoevsky's message for his reader and for all of Russia is that the Holy Spirit despite the ever presence of evil will stay forever among humans. Alyosha and Grushenka are free beings and because they are free they are more open to the Holy Spirit than are others. Rakitin does not get it but just after Grushenka speaks, Dostoevsky makes sure we get it. He writes:

"Rakitin wondered at their enthusiasm. He was aggrieved and annoyed, though he might have reflected that each of them was passing through a spiritual crisis such as does not come often in a lifetime. But though Rahitin was very sensitive about everything that concerned himself, he was very obtuse as regards the feelings and sensations of others — partly from his youth and inexperience, partly from his intense egotism."

The "eternal truth" has become a living spirit in the souls of Alyosha and Grushenka because they love one another with a spirit that is holy because it does not seek advantage over or pleasure from one another's body. All love that is completely selfless comes from God. Alyosha, revived spiritually, returns to the monastery, prays soulfully, and receives from God a holy joy in his soul that he has never felt before and that he is certain comes from God. But Grushenka, even touched by the Holy Spirit, rushes off in a carriage to meet in a nearby town with the man who seduced and abandoned her five years before. The Holy Spirit frees our spirit but we are free after experiencing it to accomplish either the "eternal truth" or the "earthly truth". This freedom in Grushenka's soul sends her off on a path towards what seems to be to her advantage. Dimitri Karamazov interrupts her meeting with her officer and during several turns this way and that way in the drama "something in Grushenka's face struck him suddenly and at the same moment a new idea flashed into his mind — a strange new idea!" He concocts a plan to outwit his rival that eventually that night leads Grushenka to realize the foolishness of seeking to cure the emotional wound she received in her past by a new relationship with her seducer. The look Dimitri has seen on her face comes from a spirit of love in her soul that should not be there. It is a holy love, the "eternal truth" that will unite them forever. A short time before when Dimitri was about to interrupt the meeting at the hotel between Grushenka and her former lover, he almost committed suicide because of his despair and hopelessness. Now just after discovering the new look in Grushenka's eyes directed at him, "There was a sort of boldness, a sudden confidence shining in his eyes. His face had looked very different when he entered the room an hour before." Dimitri's rival leaves the hotel for good. During a wild party with drinking, singing and dancing, Grushenka finally let's Dimitri know with words what he already knows in his heart, that she is his and he hers forever. Dimitri holds her and kisses her on her lips. He carries his prize to a room in the hotel and lays her on a bed. The two are free to make love but both decide that they will not and postpone it. Grushenka has been going over in her mind the love she has felt for Dimitri's rival. She is disgusted with herself for having experienced it because compared to what she feels now it seems to have been false. "Do you know, Mitya, I shall go into a nunnery. No, I really shall one day, Alyosha said something to me today that I shall remember all my life...Wicked as I've been, I want to pray, Mitya...Every one in the world is good. Every one — even the worst of them." A short time later, a police captain and other policemen and officials arrive at the hotel and announce to Dimitri that they are arresting him for the murder of his father, a crime that he did not commit even though many pieces of evidence that the police possess prove using reason and logic that he did. Thus the "earthly truth" enters the drama dominating the lives of Dimitri and Grushenka even though they have found within themselves the "eternal truth", the presence in their hearts of a holy spirit.

Only a complete communication between all men that reaches in the soul the Christ-like love of the Holy Spirit can create the kingdom of God, eliminate evil in the world and destroy the doubt in the soul about God that tortures humanity. Teaching Russia and all the Russians that they should seek the kingdom of God is what the great novel, *The Brothers Karamazov*, is about. Dostoevsky knew better than anyone because of the great spiritual trials in his life and because of his painful struggles to live freely that the Holy Spirit is present among us. It did not concern him greatly as he wrote *The Brothers Karamazov* and died shortly afterwards that the kingdom of God was not yet the only kingdom on earth because he was certain the kingdom exists already within us and that none of our false human kingdoms will ever be strong enough to kill it. Every time we experience a Christ-like love in ourselves it comes not from ourselves but from a Holy Spirit that mysteriously fills us with a foreign heavenly spirit that is also our true self. All love that does not contain any desire to possess another body or things in the world comes from God. If we ourselves communicate this love to another we create the kingdom of God on earth. Christ said that whenever two are together in his name he is among them. We must dare to escape a false self and break through without using logic and reason and without the restraints imposed on our freedom by human knowledge to our true self. This can not happen by following the path of rational morality or rational knowledge. The peace of the Holy Spirit comes only from a free spirit to a free spirit. Christ told his disciples that he must leave them and submit to crucifixion in order to leave behind for them on earth the Holy Spirit. The Holy Spirit is ours but it should never be only mine. I must share it with others or receive it from others to create as a real presence in the objective world the kingdom of God. What will Alyosha do with the holy spirit he received from the elder Zossima? Zossima commanded him that he must go out and live married in the world after his death because that is the way his holy spirit lives and spreads. The Holy Spirit needs the world as much as the world needs the Holy Spirit. For Dostoevsky freedom is divine because it alone leads to a spirit that is true because it comes from God.

Part Two

Berdyaev

1

Dostoevky's creations pulse through his pages as if there were no ground below their feet. His characters seem out of touch with themselves. We sense that their relationships with others have no solid basis. The plots in some of his novels go on for hundreds of pages even after the main climax has been reached. The struggle of his characters to find an authentic identity usually fails. Yet they are so human and so vulnerable and so wounded that they can not prevent slipping mysteriously into someplace in their being where God and the devil lie hidden. Leo Tolstoy could never have invented a Stepan Trofimovich, a false man in a false marriage. Tolstoy's characters are finely molded into fixed human forms so authentically alive that freedom from their own being is impossible. They are nothing other than what they are. Dostoevsky's characters are enslaved in a form of being so fundamentally flawed that freedom itself is part of their very nature. They are something other than what they are. Dostoevsky experienced the same groundlessness as his creations, the same humiliations and sufferings, the same feelings of inauthenticity, the same vulnerabilities but he never tried to save himself from the terrible enigmas he met in his own being by clutching for salvation and security at ideal realities. He held on stubbornly to only what was human in himself and in his creations and finally in his last work, *The Brothers Karamazov*, he found a religious freedom in himself that he reached because he had never given up searching for God in man. Nicholas Berdyaev devoted his life to this freedom of Dostoevsky that exists because God and man find their true nature only in true humanity.

Nothing can eliminate the human freedom in our being. Christianity in the Middle Ages tried to keep it idle but it expressed itself nonetheless in outbursts of evil and sin and in heretical doctrines. During that period, creative human expressions with their sources in human freedom are largely unknown. Theater in the Middle Ages developed using plots derived from religious stories like the temptation of Adam and Eve. Dramatic performances with Adam and Eve and the serpent as the main persons of the drama were presented before the doors of churches. Later there were miracle plays with divine beings from scripture appearing miraculously to create happy endings. We have few personal or autobiographical works surviving from the Middle Ages. The writings of Abelard in the twelve century about his love interest in Héloïse is one exception that proves the rule. Chivalry was not personal and individualistic. Knights were chivalrous following a code of behavior that derived from religion. Dante's great poem, *The Divine Comedy*, is the main expression we have of personal and human experience but people are all revealed within a religious context in either hell, purgatory or paradise. Nonetheless, like Shakespeare and Dostoevsky, Dante finds the divine only among forms of God's creation that are distinct from God. He does not seek the divine directly but indirectly in human nature. Dante's humanism is easily distinguishable from the later humanism of the Renaissance. Dante wrote in the 13th century and during the early years of the 14th century. The Renaissance takes place later in the 14th century and during the 15th century because humanity could no longer restrain the human freedom living within it. Humanity had to use it. Creativity had to burst out taking personal and individualistic forms because human freedom made it not only possible but necessary.

Shakespeare felt the need to create for his dramas every kind of person possible across a wide range of human possibilities. He was not guided like Dante by religion but neither was he irreligious or against religion. If anyone can read all his dramas and actually experience what he expresses in each of his persons, such an experience would reveal a world that must have God in it. No one can say that Shakespeare's dramas are only human. He reveals the human so completely and so freely that it becomes in its totality divine. Dostoevsky does the same. Hundreds of individuals of all sorts swarm together in his works. His concentration on the purely human in such a great variety of persons and situations is in its totality also divine. Shakespeare and Dostoevsky both create persons of one kind in one work and then create someone with the opposite character in another work. Raskolnikov is extremely rational with willfulness repressed and the Underground Man is extremely willful and irrational. Shakespeare likes to create a scene and create an antithetical scene right after it and then a new scene that develops and a new antithetical scene and so forth. In Hamlet he goes so far as to create in one work not just one Hamlet but several. Hamlet in the first act is a boyish mystic talking to a ghost. Soon he is an intelligent and witty young man in revolt against authorities and pretending artfully to be mad. Then he craftily manages a group of actors in order to reveal by the scene he has them play the guilt of his uncle. Another Hamlet is a misogynist who causes the death of Ophelia. Another a son who bravely endures as a more mature man a confrontation with his mother about her marriage to his uncle. Finally through new changes and travel abroad he becomes the totally new practical and rational Hamlet of the final act who declares before his fatal duel "readiness is all". Shakespeare's genius makes it impossible to say simply what the play means and over the centuries critics have expressed about it many contradictory meanings. Dostoevsky creates so many Russian characters so different from one another that he makes Russia itself seem divine since it is impossible to state using his characters as models what being an authentic Russian means in some precise way. Shakespeare and Dostoevsky make multitudes of humans act and speak before us without allowing any of them to adopt some final and definitive human form and say some final word. They can only "strut and fret their hour upon the stage" without ever speaking a final word or still less reaching "the last syllable of recorded time".

Berdyaev immersed himself in countless cultural and philosophical experiences so extensively that we can think of him as transfering Dostoevsky's passion to find God and freedom in humanity to the world of human culture and human thought. Berdyaev's great spirit provided him with a lifelong passion strong enough to experience and make his own inwardly, spiritually and mentally, all the cultural and intellectual experiences of renaissance and modern western culture as well as a great deal of what was created in previous centuries. Little escaped his free spirit and he experienced everything vitally and passionately making each new cultural or philosophical experience his own and then transcending it to new cultural or philosophical experiences. He believed that freedom, freedom in all areas of life, was the only goal truly worthy of a human being's full devotion. The freedom expressed by Dostoevsky in his Grand Inquisitor scene became the fundamental philosophical and religious basis of his free spirit. As a philosopher he was unique because he fought within himself to keep his spirit free even while experiencing thoughts opposed or hostile to his position. He made the thoughts of other creative thinkers his own and usually retained some portion of them, however small, when he exposed his own thoughts altered somewhat but still authentically his own. He is the only Christian writer who succeeded in grafting onto his Christian spirit parts or elements of most of the great thoughts and profound experiences of Western Culture. He lived in a period, 1874 to 1948, when providing oneself with a European culture was the goal of the educated in Europe and many other parts of the world. People experienced with their emotions and their spirit the works of great thinkers, writers and artists and used their own thoughts gleaned from exposure to well-known creative works as a means of communication with one another. European cultural experience shared by many people from various countries added a rich dimension for communication beyond mere language. No persons in the period enriched themselves with European culture more extensively than Nicholas Berdyaev. And he was enriched deeply by his native Russian culture also.

Other Russians voyaged deeply into European culture as did Berdyaev and, speaking generally, although some abandoned Russian culture and became culturally European, many absorbed European ideas and cultural experiences in order to oppose them and assert some new cultural expression based in their native Russian culture. No Western European of the 19th century could create a *Crime and Punishment* with a Raskolnikov testing the value of European rationalism by murdering two innocent women. But Raskolnikov had absorbed deeply within himself European cultural ideas. They had become his own and they called forth in him a uniquely Russian reaction. The Underground Man also deals with European ideas that have influenced him and that he rudely rejects. In *The Possessed* Dostoevsky reveals his contempt for the completely Europeanized author, Karmazinov, representing the actual writer Turgenev. Berdyaev also opposes European values but he makes them partly his own finding some limited value in each influence he undergoes. He believed the spirit of God was in everyone and he found some expression of the divine in the works of all the great creators of western culture. Influenced profoundly by Dostoevsky and especially by the freedom he expressed in the Grand Inquisitor scene, he makes freedom the basis of his personalistic philosophy and boldly goes both along with him and radically beyond him in the search for God in man. In 1945 when he was three years from his death and an exile in Paris going through difficult circumstances, he wrote, "In true humanity not only is the nature of man revealed but God Himself is revealed also."

2

Spirit was the fundamental power in Berdyaev's being and he believed the spirit of God entered his spirit and participated in it when he acted creatively and freely. The spirit of God, even though it lives in a realm completely different from anything human, nonetheless enters history and takes part in human sufferings and struggles. God's entrance into human life is a free act that arrives mysteriously and as if from out of nowhere. Men participate in the divine when they free themselves creatively from the slavery that subjugates them to forms of life that are objective and near to godlessness. Berdyaev was not religious or spiritual in the sense that those words are understood in western Christianity. God was a spirit who united with Berdyaev's spirit in his acts that were truly free, truly human and truly creative. He was not interested as a believing Christian primarily in the soul but in the spirit alive in his soul. He assumed that every living being lived and breathed because this same spirit that is God is also within them although often hidden and unknown to them because of their fallen and debased human condition. He could not conceive as an Orthodox Russian Christian that spirit was something abstract and completely removed from any human being of any condition with any kind of behavior or belief. Spirit was beyond everything and at the same time in everything. The elements of Christianity that the west considered most important, grace, freedom from sin, good works, faith, penitence were secondary. Berdyaev is a Russian Christian. He is before everything else interested in spirit, both divine and human.

The human world of falsity and slavery is a prison that men must escape to find the truth. Thought does not reach truth unless it is accompanied by feeling and the whole person is involved in the thought. Man must break through what is accepted as normal and truthful to reach a true understanding of God but this happens rarely because men limit themselves through egotistical prejudices and the acceptance of only objective and rational standards as guides to the real. But man cannot prevent himself from expressing spirit even if he has contempt for spirit as was the case, for example, with Karl Marx. Berdyaev was influenced by Marx and was a socialist revolutionary in his youth, but even when he later opposed Marx and Communism he still found something of value for the spirit of human freedom in Marx's criticism of capitalism. Capitalist society like all societies have strong elements in their makeup that are anti-human and anti-divine and at their worst nothing but instruments producing human slavery. Slavery tries to govern everything including human knowledge and the knowledge of God. Berdyaev had a keen rational eye that quickly saw slavery in all its forms and a strong and free spirit willing always to meet face to face the best and the worst in men. His deep faith in God taught him that there were no atheists. He found the spirit of God in protests against God because at bottom protesters were seeking a higher and more truthful form of God than the one forced on them by enslaved religious doctrines. This point of view allowed him to find some expression of the truth of Christianity in most of the great philosophers and writers that he criticizes in his writings. All the great creations of ancient and modern western culture had value for him because the spirit of God is present in all human creations. Berdyaev expressed the greatness of his spirit by assuming throughout his life the titanic task of reconciling all of western culture with Christian culture. He was convinced that it is impossible to doubt the reality of religious experience and that such experience should be sought in the creative works of men and used to enrich Christianity. Reading no matter what writing of Berdyaev usually gives a believing Christian a positive spiritual boost and his writings strengthen and inspire the souls of those leaning towards Christian belief.

For him there were no atheists. There were only idolaters devoted to notions of what is real in human experience that are neither truly divine nor truly human.

A real man must be like God because the divine is within him. If we cannot find anything at all divine in our neighbor, then what is he? Is he simply an animal? In that case how can we respect him, as we wish, since if we see him merely as an animal then he seems lower in value than we and his debased condition gives us a false sense of our superiority. Humanness for Berdyaev is the real and only basis for true religion. He believed that God himself demands that men be human. Berdyaev was bound to the human because he was always able to find personhood even in the most debased human. When we say we are all human we deny that we are each of us profoundly unique. We do not wish to recognize a distinct personhood in every man and woman and also in any animal. In Berdyaev's thought it is absurd to think that personhood is the result of some natural process that develops in a soulless human nature. Personhood is a direct sign from God that a human has something born in him that is more than human. God needs man and man needs God. Man is not man without God and he condemns himself to nothingness if he uses his freedom to cut his dependence on God. Man is perfectly free to revolt and to try to live on his own. But even in his revolt for Berdyaev he cannot rid himself of God because his nature is God-given and it remains divine-human no matter how greatly he debases it. But God for him is also one path to freedom. There is no such thing as slavery to God. God frees men because he creates in each a personhood freely given and unique. Man cannot destroy a divine element in his personhood even though to Berdyaev it was obvious that man enslaves himself in all kinds of idolatrous relationships. Even scientific humanism is idolatrous. Anything that sets up some standard for knowledge that is not God-based falls into some form of slavery. But we should not think that Berdyaev was totally against science. He was not totally against anything. He found bits of divine humanism even in science because for him any human creativity that comes close to the truly human comes close also to the truly divine.

He never gave up his belief in the divine-humanity of Christ. He was not a liberal influenced by nineteenth and twentieth century science who abandoned Christianity to live freely. Everything he wrote about Christianity and God however was about liberating Christianity from false and enslaving ideas. Only a free Christianity that liberated men from false religious and humanistic ideas and restored man to his God-given nature was of value. The human pre-exists as a reality in God before the creation of man. Man in the world must either rise or fall. He either raises himself to a new level of being, to a new divinely-shaped ego, or he freely plunges himself down to some level of beastiality. Every man has more than one ego. He has a divine-human ego created by God in him before his birth that he can reach through free thought and free creativity. He has also the possibility to create for himself a human ego that is godless and adapted to the objective world, a world of spiritual slavery and of various other kinds of slavery. Human religion itself is enslaved by false ideas. Men have killed and tortured other men because of hunger for power over others urged on by false religious ideas. Kirillov and Shatov in *The Possessed* of Dostoevsky are examples of men enslaved by false ideas about religion. Kirillov is so enslaved by an idea that it drives his false ego to destroy him by his suicide. A new Christian consciousness must free Christians from false religious ideas and from false human egos and allow them to deal freely and creatively with their own humanity and the humanity of all men. A need for power is one of the principal scourges of humanity. Only by assuming a divine-human humanity can humanity free itself from the cruelty that emerges in religious, economic, national, political and family expressions of power. For Berdyaev the spirit of God and the true spirit of men is beyond and superior to all forms of power and all the various egos men create for themselves falsely. Man should climb out of the hole where he lives. He can begin rising as soon as he discovers that the spirit of God has been in him since before his birth and is within him still. He has only to give up forever the ego he created for himself and be the free ego that God created.

3

Nicholas Berdyaev was born in Kiev, Russia in 1874 to an aristocratic family. His mother, Princess Kudashev, was half-French related to French aristocracy through her mother Countess Choiseul. She was educated in Paris, spoke French as her main language and never learned to write Russian properly. Young Nicholas grew up among members of a cultural and economic elite. Although throughout his adult life he experienced problems supporting himself economically, he never escaped impressing people as an aristocrat. Even when living in exile in Paris in a state of near poverty, people believed he was wealthy. The world he lived in as a child and a very young man is gone. He remembered as a child visiting Vienna, a city that pleased him greatly. Vienna in the 1880s with its grand imperial buildings, its beautiful theaters, its cafes filled with well-dressed people and horse-carriages passing in the wide streets! Vienna that knew nothing at all of global warming and pollution and of a world war still thirty years away! Nicholas found it beautiful and he could not have been untouched by its rampant bourgeois optimism. Four times in his life he was arrested and imprisoned, twice by the Tsarist government which exiled him to Siberia and twice by the Communist government which exiled him to Western Europe. But Vienna in the 1880s taught neither Nicholas nor the Viennese anything about their future. It was a beautiful city and it made people there feel the future was good and golden. Nicholas' father was the head of a state bank in Kiev, had solid relationships with the leading men in business and government, and came from a long line of gallant and courageous men who had served their Tsar mainly in his military. When the Tsar's police came to arrest Nicholas for revolutionary activity, they feared disturbing his father and waited nervously until the elder Berdyaev allowed them a proper entrance to his presence to arrest his son. When Nicholas arrived in the village in Siberia where he was exiled, he entered the best hotel and informed them that he required their best room. Nicholas Berdyaev was aristocratic socially and in his character.

Yet he had personal contacts with ordinary Russians early in life. Even though he was an enemy of nationalism, his relationships with ordinary Russians marked his spirit profoundly. He was exiled from Russia in 1922 along with groups of upper-class persons and had relations in exile with elite Russian social circles in both Berlin and Paris. They universally denounced the anti-Tsarist communist government in power in Moscow. Berdyaev, although an anti-communist, boldly confronted all of them challenging their hopes of restoration of a Tsarist government as an illusion. He asserted that he supported the present political situation in Russia because it was the will of the Russian common people. As a child he was given a nurse, a nyanya, who was born a serf. He grew to love her deeply. He had a skill for riding horses well and at nine a Cossack used to come to his house who taught him to ride Cossack style. They used to ride together outside of town delighting in galloping. He grew up with a young man from the common people as a member of his family. But the aristocratic side of his character and the influence of his social connections never left him. His aunt, Countess Branitskaya, owned the town of Belaya Tserkov, about one hundred and fifty thousand acres in the district of Kiev, and palaces in Warsaw, Paris, Nice and Rome. She was related to the royal family. Her summer residence near Kiev had a magnificent park laid out in a baroque manner and together with the town was something like a feudal duchy. The countess was a close friend of Nicholas' mother and his family stayed at her residence often. When there as a child, Nicholas was provided with a carriage and two ponies which he used to drive into the woods to search for mushrooms. A coachman in Polish livery sat behind him. He continued to visit his aunt's residence even in later years as a student who was a Marxist and professed social-democratic convictions. His aunt in her charming way was always kind to him. He used to stay with her for a month or so to enjoy a period of quiet study.

Berdyaev's thought always has its foundation in the aristocratic world he inherited as well as in the broad and partially submerged underground world of the common Russian people. He learned to speak both French and German fluently as a child and this might make one suspect that his exile to Berlin and later to Paris was a fairly pleasant relocation. It was not. He did not want to leave Russia and the Russian people whom he loved. His thought comes from what is real beyond and above what is common in life, from spirit, which he came in contact with partly because of his detached and elegant circumstances as an aristocrat. But his thought is also grounded in the vast unlettered, unthinking, uncultural swaths of irrational life as experienced by common Russians. He plunged into this life and made it a dynamic element of his being and of his thought. He was always struck positively by a sentence of Dostoevsky, "An aristocrat is irresistible when he goes in for democracy". But his patriotic and spiritual oneness with the deep and unexplored regions of the Russian soul was not the result of some fanciful thought in a sentence but of a life-long existential journey into the roots of humanity's being. He was living in Paris when it fell to the Germans in 1940. When he had lived beginning in 1922 for two years in Berlin, he had friendships with Germans and some of these continued in Paris as Germans governed the French. Culturally speaking, he was partly culturally French and partly culturally German. As a Russian national living in France he was not obligated to choose one side or the other. Then in 1941 Germany invaded Russia and at once in an explosion the fire of Berdyaev's love for Russia burst out visible to everyone. He divided everyone absolutely and outspokenly into either the good who supported the Russians or the evil who supported the Germans. The fire in his soul made him completely blind to any middle ground. The soul of Russia was on trial before the eyes of the world and for Berdyaev it's death would have been his own soul's death. Russia's soul was the greatest part of Berdyaev's soul and his whole mighty spirit during the German war in Russia howled to the world that anyone who helped the Germans was trying to kill something immortal.

His house in Kiev was at the top of a great hill and down below were the homes of the merchant class. This class, the middle-class or the bourgeoisie, was not as well developed in Russia as in Western Europe but its worldview and its values had elements that influenced Berdyaev's thought as they inevitably influenced all thinkers. He was opposed spiritually, intellectually, politically and religiously to the claims of the bourgeoisie that they were a universal class whose way of life, grounded in a practical and rationalistic view of what was real, must inevitably be adopted by everyone. Berdyaev, an aristocrat with a deep positive attachment to the irrational life of ordinary Russians, was as far from being a bourgeois as is possible. He not only rejected the bourgeois way of life but also the way of life of the aristocratic society in which he was born. He found balls dull, refused to act like the other cadets in his elite military school, and saw early with his clear rational eyes that there was no sound basis for the Russian aristocracy and that it was not much more than an association of rich snobs. His refusal to live enclosed psychologically in a snobbish and egotistical elite aristocratic society was certainly not a choice a true bourgeois would make! Both in Russia and Western Europe men of the bourgeoisie were avidly using their wealth to buy aristocratic titles and to worm their way into aristocratic society as false aristocrats. But another early choice that Berdyaev made was that his way of life was to be that of a philosopher, a man of ideas, and this meant that he had to infiltrate into his spirit the ideas of many philosophers, like Descartes and Kant, whose ideas about the real contributed to the intellectual foundations of the bourgeois worldview. Berdyaev as the result of some bourgeois influence never gave up his view that man was a rational animal. Dostoevsky in *Crime and Punishment* and in *Notes From the Underground* criticised and opposed bourgeois rationalism. Berdyaev's spirit told him he had to use the irrational part of his nature fully and he accepted Dostoevsky's criticism wholeheartedly. But he remained a rational thinker even though the vast sweep of his spirit travelled far beyond the limits of bourgeois rationalism which he considered petty and absurdly limited. He understood Descartes correctly. The French philosopher Descartes criticised all knowledge before his time and concluded, like a good bourgeois, that truth can only be expressed in some rational or mathematical mode. But this did not mean for Descartes that only some rational reality exists. For him as well as for the German philosopher Kant a whole vast area of reality exists even though it cannot be forced into some rational or mathematical configuration, into some *modo geometrico* as in Spinoza's thought, and cannot therefore be expressed in the limited rational forms of bourgeois truths. Berdyaev went after the expression of this irrational side of life as spirit. Spirit was what was true in God's life and man's life and spirit is both rational and irrational.

4

He experienced a conversion when still young that was the most important experience of his life and whose influence never ceased to affect him deeply throughout his life. The experience taught him in one spiritual instant that there is meaning to life and that his life had meaning. This was not a purely intellectual or mental experience nor was it like some common stereotypical version of a conversion as some ecstatic rebirth of the soul. It was intellectual, it was mental, it was a rebirth of his soul but it was above all else a revelation within him that life means something because spirit is real. The reality of spirit meant that his own individual life meant something because of the revelation of a spirit within him that never could be taken from him by anything or anyone in the objective world around him. There was nothing transcendent and beyond and above about the experience. It happened instantly within him. He experienced in something like a spiritual split second that the truth exists and that his own self must always genuinely exist truthfully when seeking truth freely and that truth and spirit and his own self are the same thing. Berdyaev had already been profoundly influenced by the passionate search for truth in the lives and works of Tolstoy and Dostoevsky. Here we have in Berdyaev's conversion a direct connection to Dostoevsky's belief that God desires freedom for man and that freedom is the true path to genuine religious experience. Up to this critical moment, Berdyaev felt no significant religious influence from exposure to the Russian Orthodox faith. It was something that his aristocratic class accepted automatically. But Nicholas already had interiorized Dostoevsky's notions of freedom and Tolstoy's courageous search for some new religious truth that would inspire new revolutionary religious practices opposed to the religious practices of the Russia of his time. Berdyaev's conversion was prepared by these two great Russian spirits. He did not experience his conversion as having anything to do with accepted religious practices. It was simply a profound good that revealed to him in one instant a pure and momentous truth. Berdyaev knew at that instant that spirit was real and that he was real because spirit was within him.

Berdyaev's conversion gave him suddenly a kind of wordless and thoughtless understanding unrelated to human logic that he was independently of everything that was and this was that he was was eternal. In one instant he became spirit and, since he could not remain spirit, in the next instant he felt human again and felt now for the first time that his human nature was divinely good. He was still himself but he was no longer the himself that he was an instant before and yet indeed he was this himself converted to a new himself. It is of the nature of the self to assert itself. A self that reveals itself to a self is a totally illogical event but Berdyaev experienced the revelation and because it was a real experience and also illogical he knew it must be spirit and that he in his essence was spirit. All his life afterwards he never sought knowledge as it is normally understood and sought instead a creative liberation in his thought that would lead himself and his listeners or his readers to spirit. He would also lead them towards freedom because he knew that the spirit he discovered within himself was part of him without diminishing his freedom. Spirit was itself freedom and it could be discovered only by freedom. Before his conversion and still a young man, he had broken all connections with normal societal beliefs, thoughts and practices. He respected and loved his parents but the idea of a family being some sort of natural and normal part of life was foreign to him. He had begun reading philosophical works and had already busied his spirit combating the ideas of others and asserting his own instead. He thought current thoughts like Freud's exposition of the oedipus complex were absurd. He was thoroughly grounded in the complex and passionate dramas of Dostoevsky and he along with Tolstoy provided

Berdyaev the entrance to a world that could not be experienced fully except by a truly free spirit. Kirillov in Dostoevsky's *The Possessed* went nowhere in spirit because he was enslaved by an idea. Shatov was entrapped by false ideas but his spirit was freer than Kirillov and it was breaking towards freedom. Sonya offered Raskolnikov the possibility of a Christian conversion but he was not free enough in spirit to reach beyond his rational ego and seize a new divine ego that was more truly his human ego than the one he himself had created. Berdyaev never felt at home and comfortable in any world, either the world of his childhood and earlier manhood or the world of his future. He read that Dostoevsky's Grand Inquisitor, looking menacingly at a silent Christ, said God demanded that man be free and he took it to heart. Spirit was his reward. He discovered spirit by first freeing his being from everything entrapping his spirit and suddenly in an instant spirit revealed to him that it was real and that he was real too. For Berdyaev the path from freedom to spirit and back again to freedom became a path rooted in his being. In all his writings he tried to get his readers to discover within themselves the same path. Here are his own words on the subject, "True human-ness is likeness to God; it is the divine in man. The divine in man is not 'the supernatural' and it is not a special act of grace; it is a spiritual principle which is in man as a particular reality...In order to be completely like man it is necessary to be like God. It is necessary to have the divine image in order to have the human image...It is not man who is human but God. It is God Who requires of man that he should be human."

This is the fulfillment of Dostoevsky's new revelation to humanity about God in the Grand Inquisitor scene: God demands that man choose to be free because this is the only way he can reach his true nature which must be both divine and human to be true. This true nature is also the true self. To discover our true self we must become in our very being the spirit of God which alone makes our human self genuine. Let's repeat Berdyaev's notion that to be genuinely human our nature must be divine-human, "In order to be completely like man it is necessary to be like God. It is necessary to have the divine image in order to have the human image. It is not man who is human but God. It is God who requires of man that he should be human." And he says further that there is something particularly Russian about this new religious point-of-view, "There are native traits of Russian religious philosophy which distinguish it from Christian thought in the West for... realizing in himself the human image man realizes the divine image. In this lies the mystery of God-manhood, the greatest mystery of human life. Manhood is God-manhood." Our true human image is our true self because it is also a divine image and God-manhood realized is freedom.

This Russian or Orthodox religious point-of-view is true because it is based on a discovery Berdyaev made through his conversion that is true universally. No one should try to fix and limit conversion of any type associated with any religion or religious system of belief in some rational and logical description *in modo geometrico.* But that said, we have enough information about religious conversions from Christian and other religious sources to name Berdyaev's conversion a first conversion. Other persons of religious fame, specifically Blaise Pascal and Saint Augustine, experienced most likely first and then second conversions. Berdyaev tells us that his conversion did not happen because he "assented to some specific truth or truths, or some explicit belief, but by virtue of a decision to dedicate my life to the search for truth and meaning. To seek truth is, indeed, in a significant sense, to have already found it, and to arrive at a conviction concerning the meaning of life implies a state of being imbued with that meaning. St. Augustine and Pascal have, in their own way, borne witness to this paradoxical experience." Sonya in *Crime and Punishment* tried to convert Raskolnikov by influencing him to believe that Christ was the son of God. Had he done so, he would also have discovered by a kind of instantaneous rush of spirit to the forefront of his being that his life was imbued with meaning. He would have discovered a completely new Raskolnikov just as Berdyaev discovered a completely new Berdyaev. These new personas would be full of meaning because they would have discovered nothing more than themselves, or, to put it in terms of Orthodox or Russian beliefs, they would have discovered the divine-human nature that they were and that they had been even before their birth. Berdyaev writes of his conversion, "As a result of my spiritual reorientation I acquired a new inner strength. My whole life changed and I felt as if carried on the wings of some spiritual rapture. I had found a sense of spiritual stability, of the unshakable spiritual ground of life…" This speaks to the universal nature of a first conversion. It is fundamentally a strengthening of the self that comes as if from nowhere. Whether it results from a decision to seek truth or to believe in the divine-human nature of Christ, it brings to a person a spiritual rapture that convinces him he has reached the truth that he is real eternally and, yes, that he himself is like Christ both divine and human.

But there is a second conversion. Both Saint Augustine

and Blaise Pascal experienced the same kind of first conversion as did Berdyaev. Pascal had a near death experience in a carriage accident that turned himself, and his sister, by his influence on her, into serious Christians. But he wavered in his commitment to Christian conduct and lived a worldly life until a few years later when he received a mysterious deep experience of love and grace that he was certain came from God. He wrote down a description of his experience that survives. It was not simply an experience of spirit that revealed that life had meaning and restored to him his true self. It was an experience of divine love filling his being and satisfying it completely. He writes, "From about ten-thirty in the evening to about half an hour after midnight. Fire. God of Abraham, God of Isaac, God of Jacob, not of the philosophers and savants. Certitude, certitude; feeling, joy, peace. God of Jesus Christ. *Deum meum et Deum vestrum.*'Thy God shall be my God.' Forgetting the world and everything, except God. He is only found by the paths taught in the Gospel. Grandeur of the human soul. 'Just Father, the world has not known you, but I have known you.' Joy, joy, joy, tears of joy." This second conversion is clearly not just spirit but God's spiritual personhood connecting with a human soul by an infusion of divine love that leaves the mind and soul certain that it comes from God. The second conversion is both the discovery and the experience of divine grace. In Pascal's great works that gave a new voice and a new style of writing to the French language, he never tires of criticizing church officials who lived their whole life expounding the truths and duties of the Catholic religion without ever having loved God inspired by the grace that God himself infuses in the soul. Did Berdyaev ever pass through this second conversion? It is impossible to say for certain but it seems unlikely. He writes of freedom and of God's love but his Christianity lacks an emphasis on the need for grace to be truly Christian that Pascal taught and also was the main element in Saint Augustine's teaching, Augustine who was the greatest of the church fathers and whose teachings rival in importance those of Saint Paul. Saint Augustine also experienced conversion and described his experience in his *Confessions.* After years of searching for meaning in his life in all the philosophies and religions of the ancient, pagan world, he was in a feverish state of uncertainty about everything in his life. Sitting outside in a garden, he heard the voice of a child singing a song with the words, "Pick it up and read it. Pick it up and read it." He had already been influenced by Christianity and had been reading the BIble because he was close to his mother who had already converted to Christianity. He opened the Bible and read the first passage he saw which was by Saint Paul in Romans, "Not in carousing and drunkenness, not in sexual excess and lust, not in quarreling and jealousy. Rather put on the Lord Jesus Christ, and make no provision for the desires of the flesh" He describes in Latin exactly what happened then, *"Nec ultra volui legere, nec opus erat. Statim quippe cum fine huiusce sententiae, quasi luce securitatis infusa cordi meo, omnes dubitationis tenebrae diffugerunt."* It was a first conversion like Berdyaev's. *"Omnes dubitationis tenebrae diffugerunt"*, "All the darkness of doubting fled away". He had a sudden certainty as did Berdyaev, a sudden strengthening of himself, *"quasi luce securitatis infusa cordi meo"* "as if a light of security was poured into my heart". He was converted. He too like Berdyaev was strengthened by a spirit revealing itself to him that came from God. The whole translation from the Latin is, "I did not wish to read further, there was no need. Immediately even at the end of this sentence it was as if a light of security was infused into my heart. All the darkness of doubting fled away." It was another first conversion, a first conversion universally possible for humanity.

The second conversion has had strict consequences for the religious behavior of Christians. The second conversion is a revelation of God's grace and it results in a direct intimate relationship of God with an individual's soul. Saint Augustine certainly had this second conversion because he made the necessity of a regular and recurring infusion of grace in a believer's soul the basis of Christian behavior. Blaise Pascal wrote extensively about Christian theology and agreed completely with Saint Augustine as did other famous Christians who were members of the Jansenist movement among Catholics in 17th century France. For Saint Augustine and for Jansenists, sin can be conquered and salvation can be achieved only through grace. Saint Augustine wrote paper after paper in the 4th century against the new heretical doctrine among Christians named Pelagianism. It argued that grace was important but that salvation can be achieved by man's own power without grace. For Saint Augustine, this was heresy because it meant in practice that there was no sin and it meant that Jesus Christ had died on a cross to free humanity from sin uselessly and to no purpose. Berdyaev certainly accepted that evil and sin exist but his radical Russian belief that true humanity is a divine-human humanity, that the divine spirit is itself a part of the human makeup, compelled him to take a position far afield of Saint Augustine and the Jansenists. He once publicly rebuked leaders of the Russian Orthodox church because they used the doctrine of human sinfulness to put down and control common Russians politically by burdening them with a severe teaching. He did not believe in framing the human problem as sin. For him, the problem was slavery and the solution was spirit and freedom. Saint Augustine and the Jansenists sought freedom for humanity by retreating from the world and overcoming sin aided by God's grace. Berdyaev would not give up humanity's God-given divine-human nature and accept that it was enslaved only by sin. It was enslaved by everything and the only objective doctrine worthy of humanity's acceptance was that human freedom alone can reveal our divine-human nature.

5

Thinking for Berdyaev was both a dangerous and liberating experience. His thought could debase him or exalt him. But he was not afraid of the danger. Freedom always made him feel that there was divinity in humanness. He was forever digging for spirit within himself and within all men. He could never go astray because spirit itself had revealed itself to him and if he sought it again freely and creatively within himself and within other men he would find it again. His thought usually takes some form that is a spiritual or intellectual reaction to the thoughts of others. His thought breaks from the subject being considered towards a better way to understand the matter from the point-of-view of his own spirit of freedom. He does not accept any thought as final and binding. His own thoughts never satisfied him and he was always writing book after book to try to explain his position. He demanded freedom in everything, especially freedom in thought. He was dissatisfied with the great thinkers that influenced him but he sought spirit in their works because they were human and he believed spirit is always active in any kind of human creativity. He got to the essential meaning of any writer quickly and had a genius for extracting some spiritual or intellectual meaning however partial from most of them. Truth could only be true if it was founded in freedom. If it was truly free it was truly spiritual and the word of God. The word of God and the spirit of God are the same thing. They live within man. His fundamental idea is that God has linked his fate with human fate. God's spirit is irrevocably in man. God should not be sought in the infinite world of the planets above and around us. Nor should God be sought in nature which is a finite world of beginnings and ends, of causes and effects, of lives and deaths. God has left behind traces of himself in the planetary world and in nature but his real location is in a third place, man. Man's nature is forever divine-human because God has decided once and for all time that he will be nowhere else. Berdyaev is profoundly correct that man needs to be like God to be truly man. Man can never rid himself of God because God has chosen that the real and present goal of his creative activity be the eternal infusion of his own divine nature into the human nature of free men and women to make them immortal like himself. Our religious duty is to free ourselves and discover that our true nature is divine-human.

Russians during his university days in the 1890s were passionate about creating a new world with a new revolutionary way of life. Historians who characterize the period by examining only socialist and communist revolutionaries miss the point. The revolutionary spirit of the time took political shapes and demanded economic changes but the real enemy of the Russian spirit was the rationalized science-oriented dehumanized and dechristianized way of life of the European bourgeoisie. That spirit was taking control of Russia and Russians did not want it. Among students would-be Raskolnikovs were appearing as regular faces in the crowd and the voiceless underground of Russian life was seething with willful anti-rationalistic underground men. Young women refused to doll themselves up as beautiful objects because it expressed agreement with the bourgeois way of life. Young men dreamed of heroic self-sacrifices to bring to birth a happier and more perfect way of life for humanity. Berdyaev with his spirit of freedom became involved with the spirit of other young people demanding change. On one of his trips to Western Europe, he brought back to Russia revolutionary socialist-democratic pamphlets in a hidden compartment at the bottom of his trunk. He read all the revolutionary writings and began giving lectures. For a time, the writings of Marx captured his free spirit.

But he was a revolutionary before he began frequenting revolutionary circles. He tried to adapt his individual thought to that of the social revolutionaries. He had broken with most social ties to the aristocratic society he was born into and found himself living a solitary life that was a radical rupture with normal society generally and with traditional human relationships. His philosophical position was transcendent. Even in this time of his university years before his Christian period he was already not satisfied with philosophical points of view that tried to find the meaning of life in only the objective side of life where bourgeois rationality fit comfortably with rational and practical behavior. Berdyaev's spirit was always a fire within him and it needed to burn radiantly in his whole soul and his whole being instead of extinguishing itself in petty objective thoughts that suffocated human freedom.

But even with his revolutionary and argumentative nature and his strong tendency to romanticism, he nonetheless was committed to being a philosopher. Philosophy was to be the core of his life's intellectual activity. He studied with a rational and critical eye various philosophical systems. He lectured his fellow students and revolutionaries on the finer points of their doctrines and often criticized them because they lacked any connection with his own transcendent philosophical view. The truth is he never could accept that the objective world where man objectifies himself and makes himself an object among other objects could be the source of truth. Truth was beyond objective life in a transcendent spiritual reality but this reality was nonetheless in man in his spirit. As a result, even with his transcendent view, he was drawn to the revolutionary ideas of his time designed to change the objective world.

Marxism appealed to his spirit because it was rooted in a solid philosophical point of view. It also based itself on a providential view of history that was rationalized and godless but focused on the struggles of men to change the path of history and free themselves from enslavement and exploitation in the objective world. Later in life, he remained sympathetic even as an enemy of Marxism to Mark's criticism of the exploitation of workers by the bourgeoisie which he considered evil. Marx took a strong position against German Idealism. Although he was influenced by Hegel's dialectic at work in history, he rejected Hegel's notion that some ideal and absolute spirit was an historical force progressing towards some happy development in humanity's future. For Mark, only the material world had any genuine existence and the real motor of history was scarcity among men condemned by history to struggle against one another for economic dominance. For Berdyaev, spirit was active even in the objective material world but it was not the idealized and rationalized spirit of Hegel and it could not possibly originate in the material world. He rejected as did Marx Hegel's rational Absolute Spirit expressing itself in history and this helped create for a time a philosophical agreement with Marxism.

In general, spokesmen for the Russian culture of the time were against the enslaving influence of Hegelian philosophy. For Hegel, one of several German idealistic philosophers, the ideal alone constituted reality and the ideal was identical with spirit which was both abstract and rational. He observed in his great work, *The Philosophy of History*, an Absolute Spirit appearing throughout all human history and taking less abstract and various concrete forms in the cultural expressions of peoples in many periods going back to ancient Chinese culture. This spirit was rational! For Hegel, whatever is real is rational! Philosophy up to Hegel's time at the beginning of the 19th century was dominated by Cartesianism. Descartes had undertaken in the 17th century a criticism of the basis of knowledge and concluded that truth can be expressed only in rational and mathematical forms. As a result thinkers mainly tended to believe that only what could be understood and expressed rationally could be true. For Descartes however, who was a Catholic, a large area of human experience existed even though it could not be expressed rationally and judged to be true. Philosophers of the Enlightenment like Hume and Locke raised reason to a dominant and superior level above the large areas of irrational experience that had, so to speak, mixed themselves with the rational thoughts of previous thinkers.

This new position of reason established in the Enlightenment was not the humble reason of the past but a reason that bourgeois thinkers believed should rule and judge everything. It was this total reliance on reason in Western Europe that produced Dostoevsky's Raskolnikov who carried to the extreme a behavior based exclusively on bourgeois rationality. And Dostoevsky's man from the underground, an enemy of European rationality, spoke up in defense of the large area of human experience that had a genuine existence even though it could not be expressed in some rational form *in modo geometrico*. Here again is what the man from the underground said. It can be taken as Dostoevsky's response to Hegel's view (even though he might never have read Hegel!) that whatever is real is rational. "You see, gentlemen," the Underground Man tells us, "reason is an excellent thing. There is no doubt about it. But reason is only reason, and it can only satisfy the reasoning ability of man, whereas volition is a manifestation of the whole of life, I mean, of the whole of human life, including reason with all its concomitant head-scratchings…For my part, I quite naturally want to live in order to satisfy all my faculties and not my reasoning faculty alone, that is to say, only some twentieth part of my capacity for living. What does reason know? Reason only knows what it has succeeded in getting to know, whereas human nature acts as a whole, with everything that is in it, consciously, and unconsciously, and though it may commit all sorts of absurdities, it persists….man can deliberately and consciously desire something that is injurious, stupid, even outrageously stupid, just because he wants *to have the right* to desire for himself even what is very stupid and not to be bound by an obligation to desire only what is sensible." Berdyaev was a rational thinker but he refused along with the Underground Man enslavement to reason. Spirit for him played an active part in history and in the concrete practical and material actions of men but it was not purely rational as in Hegel. Berdyaev's philosophy is both irrational and rational, both transcendent and immanent. His goal was to express spirit like Hegel universally but since his thought entered into wide areas of human experience not ruled by reason and since spirit for him was not exclusively rational, he had great difficulties expressing his philosophical position. However Descartes himself would have agreed that reason relates to "only some twentieth part of my capacity for living" but he had discovered that this "twentieth part" alone could state what is true. Descartes would have said that Berdyaev entered the nineteen other parts at a philosophical risk because it is impossible to express the irrational in human experience clearly. Berdyaev accepted the risk.

The 19th century Russian critic V. Belinsky also accepted the risk. He is famous for the intellectual war he waged for the benefit of Russian culture against Hegel and his absolute rational spirit. Belinsky, before Kierkegaard's philosophical rebellion against Hegel, insisted defiantly that the freedom of the individual human to assert his individual spirit against the abstract rational spirit of Hegel was what had value. Berdyaev agreed completely with Belinsky. Mark, who also saw no value at all in Hegel's abstract spirit, fit well at least negatively with Berdyaev's and Belinsky's philosophical position against Hegel. Berdyaev lectured to revolutionaries in his Marxist period about Marx but his transcendent view made him lean towards subjectivism and idealism because even as a Marxist he was not satisfied that truth could originate in the material world. He was however profoundly interested in the appearance of truth and the divine spirit in human history. He connected with the side of Marx that focused on forces working inevitably in history towards a revolutionary new future for humanity. During his period of exile to Siberia in Volgoda, he lived a free and even happy life. During this period, he published his first book, *Subjectivism and Individualism in Social Philosophy* which was read widely among the intelligentsia and made him famous. It was discussed in Marxist circles and generally criticised negatively because it clearly expressed a tendency towards idealism and away from Marxist materialism. Berdyaev was not satisfied with the ideas in his book and was already at the time of its publication engrossed in deeper metaphysical problems well beyond idealism. After his exile, he moved to Saint Petersburg and became closely involved with members of the liberal and socialist intelligentsia. He found no meaningful intellectual agreement with either group. By the time of the failed revolutionary uprising of 1905 with its many tragic deaths, he had reached the position that social revolutions were hostile to individual freedom, which was his supreme value. He came to the conclusion that the only true revolution must be the revolution of the individual man rather than the revolutions of masses of men which result only in new forms of slavery. He broke with Marxism but he remained always a revolutionary searching for the personal revolution of his own spirit and the personal revolution in the spirit of his fellow men. It was during this period that he discovered his true philosophical identity which permanently marked all his future writings. He was a personalist. That every living being possessed a personal identity unique from every other being meant that his belief in the divine-human character of the individual man was true and expressed explicitly in personhood. God was a universal spirit that expressed itself concretely in the unique personhood of each individual. With this discovery, he now had a divine guide, universal unique personhood, to help him explore the universe within him and exterior to him at all levels. The poet Virgil guided Dante through hell and purgatory to paradise. Personhood guided Berdyaev.

6

He was directly involved in the Russian cultural renaissance of the early 20th century. In St. Petersburg he became the editor of a journal that expressed some of the new ideas and the new experiences of an extraordinary cultural period. Writers and artists were carried away by ecstatic creative experiences, by new problems and new challenges. The period was marked by independent and original philosophical thought and intense poetical imaginations and aesthetic sensibilities. It was also marked by a profound spiritual disquiet and religious searching and a widespread interest in mysticism and even occultism. Berdyaev met all the important writers and artists of the period. He was influenced and inspired by them but his insistence on total freedom in everything made him critical of everything and everyone. As a totally free spirit, he found himself isolated from any genuine communication with most of the brave spirits of the time. In a word, his freedom, his total freedom, produced a groundlessness in his thought that was criticized and found offensive by most of the St. Petersburg intelligentsia. He brooded deeply about his philosophical destiny. Despite the difficulty of his isolated position, he would not give up remaining faithful to Dostoevsky's judgement in his Grand Inquisitor piece that God demands that to be truly religious men must be free. But Berdyaev was so strongly committed to a groundless freedom independent of everything and even independent of God that his point-of-view cut him off from any connection with the concrete knowledge and the objective thoughts that other writers and thinkers relied on to form a basis for their creations and to provide a means to communicate concretely their new ideas. Freedom for Berdyaev amounted almost to a rejection of objective knowledge. He needed to join his commitment to freedom to some concrete principle in human life that was a natural ally of freedom. Since for him true creativity was divine-human, this new principle had to be also at the very center of what is divine-human in humanity. It was very simply personality. Personality was divine in origin. Men were free to refuse what is divine in their personality and become merely rational individuals. Individualism and extraordinary individuals made up the components of the cultural society in St. Petersburg that he frequented. But how many realized that their ethical duty was to transcend their individuality to reach the God-created personality that was given them by God and that could be reached only by free persons? Descartes famous statement was "I think therefore I am" (*Cogito ergo sum)*. The *cogito,* the Latin for "I think", means that thinking is the certain ground of our being. But it is an "I" that does the thinking. Our I, our self, is prior to all our thoughts. Berdyaev's conversion gave him the certainty that he could transcend his ordinary I and reach a new identity of his self as spirit. He reached a deeper sense of his individual personhood by transcending his regular individual I. He discovered what all men can discover universally, that they have been equipped since birth with a God-given personality.

This notion of divine personality is expressed along with freedom by Dostoevsky in the Grand Inquisitor scene.

Christ says nothing to the Grand Inquisitor. But his divine personal presence has had an extraordinary effect among the common people as he walked among them. They all sensed his divine personhood. His personality is hateful to the old Inquisitor because it is divine and it is able to transfer a sense of divine personhood to average people enslaved mentally by a false and crude objective knowledge and controlled by false religious ideas and laws. The *person* Christ looks silently at the old Inquisitor from his prison cell and drives him to total despair. He is so enslaved by false ideas that he can not convert to a true Christianity and reach the divine person hidden in himself even with Christ himself before him *in person*. Christ wants men not only to be divinely free like himself but also to become like himself divine persons. He comes into the world imitating a man but he knows that no human words he can speak can make the Grand Inquisitor a divine person rather than what he is, a cruel human individual. He says nothing and lets his divine presence as a person talk for him. Dostoevsky gives us *two* religious revelations in the Grand Inquisitor scene and for a time Berdyaev could relate to only one of them. Freedom jumps out at us and arouses our passion but Christ the person is also before us, silent, telling us by his silence that we are *personally* like him but we are blind to the existence of something in our personality similar to what is within him, *divine* personality. Our personhood is living objective proof and knowledge that our human being is divine in its origin.

But can the regular personality that reveals itself objectively in every individual be transcended? It is easy enough to be independent persons acting rationally in our interests but very difficult, even rationally impossible, to somehow reach deeply within our unique personality and become divine persons like Christ. Dostoevsky associates freedom and a divine person in his Grand Inquisitor scene but the old inquisitor remains enslaved by false ideas that have taken control of his being and made him personally not divine at all. He understands that Christ wants men to be free but if they reach freedom do they also at the same time reach divine personhood? Berdyaev believed this divine personhood can be discovered by a creative leap in the soul to spirit. To transform human nature to a divine-human nature in traditional Christian teaching requires a power that humans do not possess. That power is a divine love that comes completely from God and does not exist in human nature at all. It is named grace. Dostoevsky revealed grace to us in Sonya in *Crime and Punishment.* She has within her *a secret treasure* that comes from God and that she tries unsuccessfully to transfer to Raskolnikov. Dostoevsky again reveals divine grace in the silence of Christ. He is a divine person whose silence tells us that the heart of the old Inquisitor is closed to grace and that it will be of no use if the silent divine person before him sends grace to his hardened heart. His kiss on the old man's lips also reveals grace because Dostoevsky's Christ tells us by it that the Inquisitor can be moved not in his heart but only superficially by intimacy with his body. Berdyaev is not interested primarily in grace because it raises man to a divine level by a power that comes exclusively from God. He admits that he did not possess "any special gifts of grace". Personhood, the fact that each human is irreducibly a person, grounds his conception of the divine in human nature. He is interested in the "indestructibility of the human person" rather than its transcendence to divine personhood by the gift of God's grace because the new Christianity he proposes must be rooted not in the divine but in the divine-human, in God-manhood.

The search for the divine in the older forms of religion has often enslaved man by false and useless religious practices that were sometimes materialistic in their orientation. They often did not lead man to the divine at all and for Berdyaev it makes more sense to seek God in the divine-human nature of man revealed by his indestructible personhood. He writes about the person, "The dissolution of the person and the annihilation of individuality in a nameless Godhead, or, for that matter, in the whirlpool of cosmic forces, remained abhorrent to me as a betrayal of my Christian conviction concerning the God-manhood of Christ and the indestructibility of the human person. God-manhood embodies the unity and interaction of two natures, divine and human, which are one but unconfused. Man is not subsumed in God, but is made divine, and his humanity endures in eternal life". The goal of the new Christian man is not to renounce his human life to make himself by God's grace divine but to make his human life divine by freely living out on earth all the good creative possibilities of his divine-human personhood that is God-given, knowable, and indestructible.

7

Berdyaev's and Dostoevsky's insistence that freedom is a basic element of the Christian revelation is certainly within the normal bounds of Christian beliefs. Contact with God can take place personally as divine love entering the human soul. This does not enslave man in any way but instead mysteriously frees him to be completely and freely himself even while joined to God by divine love. Berdyaev's concept of man's nature being divine-human is rooted in the appearance of Christ, a divine-human being, whose sacrifice on the cross frees mankind from slavery to sin and urges man to live not just humanly but divine-humanly as Christ lived. After Christ a new element entered human nature, a divine element. No true Christian can deny his ethical duty to act to the best of his ability as a divine being. Berdyaev's reliance on personality as a divine sign in man that his human nature is uniquely personal because God created him unique with a unique personhood is rooted in the experience of Christian conversion. Berdyaev and other Christians have discovered in conversion a strengthening of themselves and a revelation of their God-given personhood on a deeper divine level. No Christian can deny that the personal born-again experience is a genuine part of Christianity. But Berdyaev does go boldly beyond traditional Christianity with his doctrine that God-manhood must make a creative leap towards God that does not result from God's influence on man but originates in the depths of man's God-manhood independently of God. This independent purely human religious creativity is possible because according to him along with the revealed truths of Christianity there exist unrevealed truths.

The existence of grace has always been the central basis for Christianity. Salvation is granted man by God's grace. Man's duty is to live as best he can in a state of grace by benefiting from the sacraments of the church, by performing with humility good works and by inflicting penance upon himself for his sins. Berdyaev does not deny the benefits of grace but he nonetheless dares to go beyond the way Christians usually relate to it. "The source of grace is in God." he writes. "Grace proceeds from on high, whilst the realization of our sinful condition proceeds from below. My question then is this: can we ascribe to grace, which redeems the frustrations and the insignificance of human existence, a quality that is not only divine but is also human, which is from 'below' as well as from 'above'? Is man justified solely by a higher power, or is he also justified by his human endeavour and creative ecstasy?" In Berdyaev's daring new development of Christianity, man seeks God's response to him not by his humility and by his human passivity but by his human creativity which like freedom does not depend for its existence on anything. Berdyaev keeps grace as coming from God but dares to believe not only that it can come freely from "above" but also that some spiritual power similar to grace can be created freely from "below".

Creativity for Berdyaev is a human response to the divine. He believed that God responds to man's creative act and that man's divine-human nature and his total freedom also require creativity to achieve a new kind of spiritual wholeness. The old kind of Christian wholeness was achieved from above by God's free act of love producing grace in a human soul. The freedom of the new revolutionary Christian is in permanent danger of a descent into sin which destroys his freedom and enslaves him to the enticements and to the pleasures of the material objective world. For Berdyaev creativity is not some "claim or a right on the part of man, but God's claim on and call to man. God awaits man's creative act, which is the response to the creative act of God. What is true of man's freedom is also true of his creativity: for freedom too is God's summons to man and man's duty towards God." Sin can never be superior to a free creative act arising in the depths of the soul of a divine-human man. This creativity should not be understood as the creativity behind artistic products in the various fine arts which for

Berdyaev are worthwhile but merely symbolic and objective products. Creativity is man's creation of man in God in response to God's creation of God in man.

Berdyaev was always adding throughout his writings the need for creativity as a key element of his thought along with freedom and personality. Creativity is the main subject of his early book, *The Meaning of the Creative Act*. It was the result of a visit to Italy. He wrote the pages about the Renaissance entirely in Italy in a state of creative ecstasy. He understood on the spot in Italy in Florence that the Renaissance was the "dawn of a new age in which the Christian soul became conscious for the first time of a will to creation". He was completely "carried away, to the point of reliving the creative urge of the Renaissance man and the affirmation of his power to make freely and out of freedom". The Renaissance was a defining moment in Western European culture but it had had almost no influence in Russian culture. Only a few select persons in the intelligentsia and the upper classes experienced the Renaissance and made it an element of their personal culture. But those who became "renaissance men" boldly announced to their fellow Russians the results of their discoveries and their dissatisfaction with contemporary culture in Russia dominated by uncreative bourgeois influences. Leontiev's grand statement about the contrast between creativity in the past and the lack of it in the present gives us the sense of how widely Berdyaev's visit to Italy opened his Russian soul to new creative possibilities. Leontiev wrote famously, "Is it not dreadful and humiliating to think that Moses went up on Sinai, the Greeks built their lovely temples, the Romans waged their Punic Wars, Alexander, that handsome genius in a plumed helmet, fought his battles, apostles preached, martyrs suffered, poets sang, artists painted, knights shone at tournaments — only that some French, German or Russian bourgeois dressed in unsightly and absurd clothes should enjoy life 'individually' or 'collectively' on the ruins of all this vanished splendor?" Berdyaev took into his soul the past splendor of creativity in the *Trecento* and the *Quattrocento* periods displayed in Florentine art, especially in Boticelli, although he did not like Italian art of the 16th century and in Rome he found Saint Peter's gigantic church "positively distasteful". In his book, *The Meaning of the Creative Act,* he wrote widely about his new religious doctrine of creativity which was related to artistic creativity but still distinctly apart from it. His religious creativity does not result as does artistic creativity in a product. His creativity is "not an insertion in the finite, not a mastery over the medium, or the creative product itself; rather it is a flight into the infinite; not an activity which objectifies in the finite but one which transcends the finite towards the infinite." His return to Moscow from Italy marked a new phase in his life. Previously he had good relationships with Orthodox Christians but now they were suspicious and hostile to his religious position because of his daring doctrine of religious creativity as expressed in his new book. Sergei Bulgakov, a priest and a leading spokesman of profound mystical truths of the Orthodox religion, in his new book, *The Light That Never Fades,* spoke of Berdyaev's defence of creativity as "demonic", "titanic", "humanistic" and nearly akin to anti-Christ. Berdyaev was the Martin Luther of Russian Orthodox Christianity. He did not believe that only the old practices of the old religion led to salvation. He proposed new practices although like Martin Luther he kept some of the old.

He believed that it is within man's creative power to transform what is finite in himself into the infinite. This creative passage from the objective material world to the subjective spiritual world can be witnessed and experienced in all of Berdyaev's writings as his free thought limited by nothing soars towards some inner contact with infinite freedom. One bridge he used to strive towards the infinite was his constant transcendence of objective forms of human knowledge. All knowledge about any subject can lead to the infinite because anyone who pursues a subject thoroughly will discover, as did Plato, that knowledge does not lead to the good in itself but to nothingness. Knowledge of any subject carried to the extreme can only reveal that there is no real and authentic knowledge because the details of any subject expand infinitely to such an extreme degree that the subject loses completely the characteristics of ordinary knowledge becoming meaningless. However this nothingness arrived at by a long and difficult search for knowledge that proves that human knowledge is false and an illusion can also be a revelation that the ultimate reality is not knowledge but God and freedom. Berdyaev pursued divine knowledge by creative leaps beyond human knowledge towards the infinite. He was not an enemy of human knowledge only because he knew that his freedom allowed him to transcend it creatively. And another means he discovered to transcend the merely human to the divine-human was human culture. All great human creations by truly free men when thoroughly accepted into the human spirit reveal that even though they come close to the infinite and the divine they ultimately do not fully satisfy the human soul's thirst for the divine. All great creations when transcended spiritually and intellectually reveal that something must exist beyond anything humans can invent, that some power must exist far beyond what humans believe finite and limited, and that nothing can ever be truly real in our human nature unless this power that we can somehow mysteriously experience in our soul is also real. Everything is possible for God and the greatest achievements of human culture when transcended may reveal this. All of Berdyaev's writings testify that he absorbed into his spirit the spirit behind great works of human culture because his underlying goal was to transcend all human culture.

Berdyaev writes, "God does not reveal to man that which it is for man to reveal to God. In Holy Scripture we find no revelation concerning man's creativity — not on account of its implied denial of human creativity, but because creativity is a matter for man to reveal. God is silent on this matter and expects man to speak. I have frequently been asked to justify my idea of the religious significance of human creativity by quotations from Scripture. I may or I may not be able to provide such justification — but in any case such a demand is evidence of a fundamental misunderstanding of the problem under discussion. It is, in fact, the concealed, rather than the revealed, will of God that man should dare to create, and such daring and creativity are a token of man's fulfilment of the will of God." And then he writes in his next paragraph, "The idea of God is the greatest human idea, and the idea of man is the greatest divine idea. Man awaits the birth of God in himself, and God awaits the birth of man in himself. It is at this level that the question of creativity arises, and it is from this point of view that it should be approached. The notion that God has need of man and of man's response to him is, admittedly, an extraordinarily daring notion; yet in its absence the Christian revelation of God-manhood loses all meaning."

Berdyaev's call to man to make a new creative response to God *on his own* is his invention of a new universal direction for spirituality. If we are to understand Berdyaev truly we must look beyond the old practices of the Christian religion. He believed that man must reveal "the concealed rather than the revealed will of God". Since he knew all the traditional religious practices and accepted them as valid, his search for the concealed will of God means that he believed he had reached a new stage in the development of Christianity in which man's "daring and creativity are a token of man's fulfilment of the will of God". He must therefore be understood as a Christian prophet of a new future of Christianity focused not on what has already been revealed but on what is secret. He calls upon man to realize a "creative work that is the fulfilment of the creator's secret will".

Dostoevsky, Berdyaev and Shestov look for God not in the exterior world that scientists examine but within man. The three Russian religious thinkers search for the divine *only* in man and this is the key to where they fit historically in the development of religious thought for they have in fact *developed* religious thought. Dostoevsky invented in the Grand Inquisitor scene a new form of Christianity based on freedom. He also described in the dramatic relationship between Dimitri Karamazov and the woman he loved, Grushenka, a new basis of union between a man and a woman. The two love one another not just naturally. They had plenty of chances to unite naturally but they could not. The Holy Spirit enters Grushenka through the personal and spiritual love she feels for Alyosha Karamazov. This gives her the strength of spirit to see that the man who abandoned her five years previously and has now returned seeking a new relationship is worthless in his inner being compared to Dimitri Karamazov. This discovery cements their natural desires for each other into a holy and eternal union by the action within them of the Holy Spirit. Dostoevsky is thus proposing a new *religious* basis for human marriage. Berdyaev is so inspired by the new religious consciousness he grasped in Dostoevsky's writings that he spent his life searching boldly for new radical developments of Christianity that can happen among men and women who are truly free. The fundamental idea in his thought is that man's being is enslaved, that man himself blocks himself off from the world of God and that he must break away from his natural being subject to the laws of nature to discover within himself his divine-human nature.

8

Berdyaev expressed spirit and freedom so fully using countless creative works of western culture as partial support for his ideas that his writings are an implicit attack on rational knowledge and on thinking using only reason of the same sort used by scientists. His philosophical position allows both rational thought and its product rational knowledge, but he makes us nonetheless certain that truth exists only far beyond the world of rational knowledge in realms of the spirit. He wrote, "Despite the established and venerable tradition of confining philosophy to logic and epistemology, I was never able to conform my mind to such a limitation or to see any possibility of true philosophical knowledge along those lines. On the contrary, knowledge appeared to me as creative understanding, involving a movement of the spirit, a direction of will, a sensitivity, a search for meaning, a being shaken, elated, disillusioned and imbued with hope. Who will deny that suffering, joy, conflict, ecstasy are sources of knowledge? Reality is, in fact, closed to those who pretend to know in a state of indifference, disinterestedness and neutrality, for they suppress the evidence of the very reality which they attempt to know. In point of fact nobody, not even Spinoza, has ever been consistent in applying the principles of such allegedly 'pure' knowledge. Philosophy signifies love of wisdom, and love implies emotion and passion. Philosophical knowledge, then, springs from the integral life of the spirit; it is preeminently spiritual experience. All the rest, the various philosophical disciplines propagated in philosophical text-books and taught at the universities are, at best, of secondary importance."

His writings do not have words anywhere that touch our souls with the deadening objectivity expressed by writers who are incapable of busting out of the prison-world we inhabit created by a knowledge that is the enemy of divine knowledge. He has inspired us to escape the limits imposed on human being by reason through creative responses to God created *on our own*. But he was never an enemy of our human knowledge even though the debased and enslaved condition of fallen humanity, according to the story related in Genesis of the fall of Adam and Eve, was the result of the terrible transition of our original parents from grace to knowledge. We must now examine the thoughts of the only major writer who ever took seriously the idea that our knowledge is an enemy that we must conquer if we are ever to reach a life with the spiritual freedom that was at the root of the souls of both Dostoevsky and Berdyaev, the thoughts of Lev Shestov.

Part Three

Shestov

In the 18th century, men like Thomas Jefferson in America and Voltaire in France, men whose wealth allowed them to live enlightened lives free from the cares and labors of common men, worshiped human reason. Rational knowledge had led to outstanding discoveries about the nature of the universe by Isaac Newton. Rational knowledge was for them the means to solve all human problems and to create a better and more perfect society in the future for the benefit of all men. Meanwhile men acted rationally to better their individual social status and through education enjoyed intellectual experiences as the result of rational thought that convinced them that reality in life was met in ideal rather than practical experiences. Towards the end of the century and during the first years of the 19th century, political revolution, the napoleonic wars, the spread of the industrial revolution changed enlightened minds in Europe to despair. Human reason was not doing its sacred job. New wealth made very few men rich and did little to lessen the miserable circumstances of most men. The middle-class, the bourgeoisie, had raised itself to riches and political power in Europe by strictly regulating its practices by reason but even the bourgeoisie at the beginning of the new century doubted that reason was able to enlighten and enrich any class of society except its own. The intellectual stage in Europe needed some new champion to step up and proclaim boldly not only that reason should still be worshiped but that everything in human history that was real was also rational.

His name was Hegel. He was a German philosopher. He wrote a remarkable book, *The Philosophy of History*, in which he elucidated the inevitable progress in history of Absolute Spirit. This spirit was entirely rational. It expressed itself in various forms throughout human history without ever expressing itself in its absolute form. It appeared in ancient Chinese history in one form and in new forms in other places in other times up to a form in the Germany of Hegel's time. Reason in the 18th century was simply reason. Hegel's reason was a reason developing in history dialectically in which negative periods were inevitable. Despite negativity and despite terrible wars and terrible sufferings, history was rational. If history employing wars or other means produced some form of society with whatever values, it was real and whatever was real was also rational. You can't argue with history. It knows what it's doing. Absolute Spirit never shows itself to men completely but it is evident in various partial expressions throughout history. If you don't like a certain form history might decide to take, be patient. Accept the reality of the form because there is nothing you can do about it since it is real and because it is real it is rational. Absolute Spirit cares nothing about particular individual men or women and its rational spirit will harm or destroy them unless they adapt rationally to whatever political and cultural form it takes in their time. Their great compensation for history's indifference to them is that whatever form history takes will inevitably be negated by some new form and so on and so forth until at the very end history's dialectical development will reach its rational purpose which is freedom.

Hegel's idealistic philosophy of historical development

gave a genuine new inspiration to the old static idealism of the 18th century. Every educated and enlightened person was an idealist. The practical, everyday life of the wretched and ignorant men and women living most of them in some degree of poverty could not possibly be taken as the source of the real. Thought, educated talk, moral enlightenment, ideals, ideal beauty was real and the vulgar struggles and sufferings of common humanity were without any real merit. But now with Hegelian dialectical thought idealism was on the move. It was progressing by negation of old forms to new forms and then new negations. Thanks to Hegel, an enlightened idealist in easy social circumstances could now look at the misery in a particular human face with a kind of mild rational and detached moral boost knowing at least through Hegel that the real structure that any society might take was rational as well as real because it was a necessary stage of history's inevitable progress. Why worry excessively about human misery? That was history's job. History was taking care of it.

Lev Shestov, as mentioned previously, wrote that Dostoevsky at the age of twenty-eight faced death from a firing squad and as a result, even though he escaped death by the Tsar's mercy, received "a second pair of eyes". Before, with his first pair of eyes, he was a member of an idealistic and revolutionary circle of men searching for some new better form of life for themselves and for Russia led by the well-known critic V. Belinsky. Belinsky, influenced as other Russian intellectuals by German idealistic philosophers like Schelling and Fichte, had strong idealistic leanings. The mass of Russians surrounding educated persons in his circle led miserable ignorant lives worse than the common people in Western

Europe. Only idealism seemed to allow an escape from pessimism to spiritual and intellectual experiences that were abstracted from common experience but nonetheless provided inner contact in the mind with something that seemed of real value. The critic Belinsky had been deeply touched by Fichte's idealism but then, along with idealists all over Europe, he had experienced the general despair in the early 19th century that reason could ever do the work of elevating humanity. Hegel's dialectical idealism proved that despite negative moments in history it nonetheless was developing rationally towards progress for humanity. Hegel promised his readers that no form that history assumed could be considered the final form, even though any form was both real and rational, because his dialectic always included a negative stage after a preceding positive stage. Belinsky was at first overwhelmingly pro-hegelian but then he discovered that Hegel was not true to his own philosophy because he had announced that the powerful Prussian state that history had formed in Germany was history's final stage. Prussia for Hegel was the absolute realization in human history of human freedom. Submission to this state because it was real and rational was freedom for each individual and there was no new negation coming in the future opposed to the Prussian state. Submission to it was absolutely necessary and submission made you absolutely free. This was too much for Belinsky. This set him thinking about the real common life of most people without any idealistic bias. He did not get "a second pair of eyes" like Dostoevsky but he used his natural eyes. He began looking squarely at all the thousands and thousands of lives of individual men and women that Hegel's abstract idealism considered of no importance at all and that Hegel had left completely out of his world picture. Dostoevsky absorbed Hegel's ideas through contact with Belinsky and he too like Belinsky began caring more about individual human lives rather than ideal hegelian abstractions. He never cared again as a writer and a thinker about anything in life that was not human and individualistic.

Belinsky had fallen in love with Hegelianism because of the new bursts of positive energy it had created in his mind and soul, but he turned completely against it. He sensed that there was something bad, even horrible, about a spirit that could take an absolute form in anything or anyone, an absolute form in the German state Prussia or an absolute form in his own being. He wanted above all to be an individual spirit and he was all at once horrified realizing that Hegel's universal rationality meant that there was no place for spiritual and intellectual individualism either in universal history or in a human person's being. Hegel's brilliant philosophical analysis of the inevitable dialectical relationship between individual consciousness and the universal presence of the substantial exterior world amounted to locking up all free individualistic being in a rationally organized prison. The prison allowed for its inmates only an experience that was real because it was also rational. Belinsky decided suddenly with his whole Russian heart and soul that he could not live without possessing a being that was absolutely free and that he had to escape from Hegel's prison even if it meant leaving reason and common sense behind him. "Even when indeed I should succeed in attaining the highest step on the ladder of development," he wrote, "I would demand that you give me an accounting of all the victims of the conditions of existence and of history, of all the victims of chance, of superstitions, of the inquisition, and so forth. Otherwise I will throw myself head first from the top of the ladder. I don't want any happiness even at no cost if I cannot be at peace about the fate of each of my blood brothers…" Belinsky, who was a well-known critic, broke the Russian intelligensia's attachment to German idealism. Before he received his "second pair of eyes", Dostoevsky had flirted with idealism but all his free individualistic creations in his works testify that he was incapable of finding reality in ideal abstractions and sought it steadfastly in varieties of human persons. His Underground Man speaks of idealism as "the love of the good and the beautiful". He prefers with his whole being spitefulness to idealism and Dostoevsky tirelessly created beings far distant from any absolute spirit. Hegel's dictum, "Whatever is real is rational" became the *bete noire* of Russian intellectuals. Lev Shestov, born in 1866 in the generation after Belinsky, criticises Hegel throughout his works and convinces us that if whatever is real is rational then we are doomed to be forever out of touch with the real.

Shestov waged unrelenting war against human knowledge and particularly against human reason which provides the strategies knowledge needs to attain victory after victory over the freedom of the human soul. Shestov wrote again and again about the poisonous effect of rational knowledge on the soul and Hegel supplied him with all the details of the origin of the poison and of how it developed. Hegel's *Phenomenology Of Spirit* proves that humans are condemned by his dialectic to renounce their individuality. Every moment of our consciousness perceives something different from what we perceived in the previous moment. Reason judges every moment of consciousness as soon to be a past moment, a moment surpassed by a new moment. Every moment that passes gives each individual knowledge of what he is really. Since his consciousness is forced to surpass each preceding moment, this activity of consciousness must convince him that the absolute spirit revealed behind each separated moment is the same spirit that constitutes his individual life. As an individual develops throughout life he escapes an instinctual and irrational life by acting more and more as an absolute spirit. He finds this same spirit in his family, in his social community, in his state and finally even in his religious consciousness. Hegel explains how through dialectical development that is inevitable in individual life rational knowledge rules every individual life and forces each life to become identical with absolute life. An individual spirit must become an absolute spirit. Knowledge says so and Hegel gives us a brilliant, expansive and detailed account in his *Phenomenology Of Spirit* of exactly how knowledge rules us. In the end Hegel, despite the continual movement of his dialect through stage after stage of moments negated and surpassed by new moments and new stages, is outlining for us permanent and fixed necessary structures controlling our being that we are powerless to escape. Paradoxically, Hegel sets up for Lev Shestov in detail after detail and brick by brick the structures of the prison that humanity must inevitably create for itself and inhabit guided by reason and human knowledge. Shestov uses his wit to try to persuade us to escape from the prison but since he cannot use reason as a weapon against reason or knowledge as a weapon against knowledge, his fight is hopeless and he admits it is so. But at least let us understand here, before we explore examples of his wit, that it is the enslaved structure of our being caused by reason and knowledge that is so shocking to him. Reason and knowledge are soldiers in the battle. The structure forced on our being, the walls of Jerico that a trumpet must miraculously make fall down, are his real enemy. The outstanding accomplishment of Lev Shestov is to have made clear to humanity that reason and knowledge have stolen from God the right to make humans certain of who they are and robbed them of the direct union with God which can alone make them truly certain and truly free.

Shestov writes, "In all times and among all peoples the natural thought of man stopped, without force, as though bewitched, before the fatal necessity which had introduced to the world the terrible law of death linked ineluctably to man's birth, of the destruction that waits for everything that appears and will appear. In the very being of man thought discovered something that should not be there, a vice, a sickness, a sin and taking that into account wisdom demanded that this sin be killed at its root, or, to express it differently, wisdom demanded the renouncement of individual being which having a beginning is condemned irrevocably to have an end....The immediate facts of consciousness discover for us the truth, existing previous to the world, eternal, unchangeable, forever insurmountable, that it is not among us and for us that true being should be sought...The law of the inevitable destruction of everything that is born and has been created, this law, discovered by an intellectual vision, appears to us as belonging to our very being."

However Shestov then boldly cites an enigmatic exception to humanity's "intellectual vision". He fearlessly opposes the biblical story in Genesis to "the law of the inevitable destruction of everything that is born and has been created". In Genesis, at the evening of each day, God contemplates the work of his creation and sees that it is *valde bonum,* very good. The man that God created, Adam, precisely because he created him, was perfect and had no default. Evil and sin did not exist in the world created by God. Sin and evil came afterwards. Scripture has an answer explaining their origin. Shestov accepted the explanation and used it as inspiration to fearlessly fight against human knowledge even though he fully understood that even religious Christians and Jews together with all rational non-believers would never accept that knowledge caused the fall of man. That however is what it says in the Jewish and Christian Bible! In the Garden of Eden, there was a tree named the tree of the knowledge of good and evil. God told Adam and Eve that they could freely eat the fruits of all the other trees in the garden but they should not touch the fruit of the tree of knowledge because the day when they ate of it they would die. We all know the rest of the story but our thought is "without force, as though bewitched" and we are unable to take the truth into our heart. The serpent told Eve that she and Adam would not die and that their eyes would open so that they would become *"sicut dei scientes bonum et malum"*, "like gods knowing good and evil".

Shestov writes, "Man let himself be tempted, tasted the forbidden fruit, his eyes opened and he became knowledgeable. What appeared to him? What did he learn? There appeared to him what had appeared to Greek philosophers and to Hindou wise men: the *valde bonum* is unjustified. Everything is not good in the created world. In the created world, and precisely because it is created, it is impossible that there not be evil, a great deal of evil, an unsupportable evil, as bears witness to us with indisputable evidence everything that surrounds us — the immediate facts of our consciousness...As soon as men became *scientes*, that is, knowing men possessing knowledge, sin introduced itself to the world, sin and evil."

The story of the fall of man in Genesis leads Shestov to a judgement about Hegel's philosophy and about the sources of philosophy "for all time". He describes Hegel as one of the most remarkable philosophers of the 19th century and someone who had absorbed in himself all of European thought since its beginnings twenty-five centuries previously. "Hegel affirms without the slightest hesitation: the serpent did not deceive man, the fruits from the tree of knowledge have become the source of philosophy for all time. And indeed it is necessary to avow it: from an historical point of view, Hegel is right. The fruits from the tree of knowledge have in effect become the source of philosophy, the source of thought for all time. Philosophers, not only the pagans for whom Scripture was completely unknown, but also Jews and Christians who considered the Bible an inspired book, all the philosophers were *scientes* and refused to renounce the fruits of the forbidden tree. For Clement of Alexandria (third century after Christ), Greek Philosophy is the 'second Old Testament'. He declares that if one could separate knowledge from eternal salvation and if it were given to him to choose between the two, he would choose knowledge and not eternal salvation. Medieval philosophy followed the same path. Mystics themselves were not any different and had the same perspective. The unknown author of the famous *Theologia deutsch* affirms that Adam would have been able to eat twenty apples and there would not have been because of it any evil. Sin did not come from the fruits of the tree of knowledge. Nothing bad can come from knowledge. From what comes the certainty of the author of the *Theologia deutsch,* from where does this conviction come to him that evil can not proceed from knowledge? He does not even ask this question. It does not even enter his spirit that we can look for and find truth in Scripture. We must search for truth only using our own reason and nothing is true except what reason admits is true. The serpent did not deceive man."

But Shestov had a weapon to use against knowledge other than Scripture. He was as deeply influenced by Dostoevsky's writings as was Nicholas Berdyaev and like Berdyaev he wrote a book about him. Dostoevsky became as passionately anti-hegelian as Belinsky. When he was a member of Belinsky's circle, he had assimilated all the fundamental ideas of Hegelian philosophy. When he received his "second pair of eyes", he displayed a philosophical clairvoyance superior to Belinsky but Belinsky had found at the time when Dostoevsky had only his regular eyes the words to express what was unacceptable for him in the doctrine of Hegel and that later became unacceptable for Dostoevsky. Let's repeat Belinsky's words: "Even when indeed I should succeed in attaining the highest step on the ladder of development, I would demand that you give me an accounting of all the victims of the conditions of existence and of history, of all the victims of chance, of superstitions, of the inquisition, and so forth. Otherwise I will throw myself head first from the top of the ladder. I don't want any happiness even at no cost if I cannot be at peace about the fate of each of my blood brothers…"

Shestov tells us how Hegel would have reacted to Belinsky's words and even what he would have said: "If Hegel had been able to read these lines of Belinsky, he would have been content to shrug his shoulders with contempt and would have declared that Belinsky was only a barbarian, an ignorant man, a savage. It is clear that Belinsky did not taste the fruits of the tree of knowledge and that he does not even suspect the existence of an ineluctable law, in virtue of which everything that has a beginning, and, precisely the people that Belinsky takes the side of with such passion, must have an end. It is useless consequently to demand an accounting (and there is no one to whom the demand can be made) about beings who because they are finite cannot pretend to be due any protection. Not only common men, the victims of chance, but even men like Socrates, Jordano Bruno and others, the greatest men, the wise, the just, have no right to any protection...The wheel of the historical process crushes them all without pity, with as much indifference as if they were inanimate objects. The philosophy of the spirit is the philosophy of the spirit precisely because it succeeds in elevating itself above everything that is finite and momentary. And, on the other hand, everything finite and momentary can take its place in the philosophy of the spirit only if it stops preoccupying itself with its own petty interests which do not deserve consequently any concern. That is how Hegel would have spoken. And in this connection, he would have referred to his *History of Philosophy* where he explained that Socrates had to be poisoned and that it was not a catastrophe at all: an old Greek died, is it worth the trouble to make so great a fuss about it? Everything that is real is rational, that is, the real cannot be and must not be other than what it is. Anyone who does not understand that is not a philosopher. It is not given to him to penetrate by the intellectual vision all the way to the essence of things. There is even more: such a one who is not able, such a one — according to Hegel — cannot consider himself a religious person. For religion, all religion, and especially absolute religion — that is how Hegel names Christianity — makes known to men in images, that is, in a less perfect way, what the thinking spirit perceives itself in the essence of being. The real content of Christian faith, says Hegel in his *History of Religion*, is therefore justified by philosophy and not by history (that is, by what is told in Scripture). That means that Scripture is acceptable to the extent that the thinking spirit recognizes that it is in harmony with the truths that it obtains itself, or, as Hegel expresses it, what he draws from himself. Everything else must be rejected.

We already know what Hegel drew from himself: whatever Scripture may say, the serpent did not deceive man, and the fruits of the forbidden tree have given us something better than anything else that can exist in the world — knowledge."

2

Lev Shestov was born in 1866 to a well-off Jewish family in Kiev, Russia. We possess an outline of his life with dates and basic facts but no biography that might give us insights into the person behind the writer. Our main hints of the person in the man are in his writings. A first and very strong impression: no writer will strike a reader as being more deeply religious than Shestov. He had an unflinching spiritual detachment that was equal to great Christian's like Saint Augustine and Blaise Pascal but he reached religious freedom by remaining faithful to a biblical power in his soul that was abrahamic and aided by no mediation between himself and God. However, strictly speaking, religion as it is generally understood is not his main theme. He writes instead about human mental and spiritual slavery caused by reason and knowledge. His most important ally against two-plus-two-makes-four is

Dostoevsky's Underground Man who uses the expression to describe his enemy in his war against all rational laws. The Underground Man admits that his desire for victory over the rational laws regulating our behavior is so hopeless that he can only "bang his head against a wall" because of his frustration. "I am not able to break through the stone wall with my head," he says, "but does this mean that the wall is an insurmountable obstacle for all eternity?" Shestov in several places writes that fighting the same fight as the Underground Man against two-plus-two-makes-four, he is powerless and can do no more than "bang his head against a wall". But Shestov is so relentless in his fight against the wall that enslaves our being that we sense there is something behind the wall worth banging our head over.

Mental and spiritual slavery was also a main theme of Nicholas Berdyaev but there is a solid difference between the way the two handled the theme. Berdyaev's spirit is always breaking with the threat to his being from slavery and finding an escape in deeper and deeper creative revelations within himself of the spirit of God and freedom. He strongly favors the irrational side of his nature but he accepts that reason and knowledge are not barriers to freedom. Shestov's spirit is always as though permanently enslaved by his own being and he is always stubbornly opposing this slavery which he is convinced is caused by reason and knowledge. The slavery of human being is the main theme of both Berdyaev and Shestov. Both wrote books about Dostoevsky and all three would agree with Blaise Pascal's description of the slavery of man's being by "an incomprehensible bewitchment, a supernatural sleepiness which points to some almighty force as its cause". Shestov puts the full quote in his book about Pascal, "Nothing is so important to man as his existence; nothing is so dreadful as eternity. And therefore it is quite unnatural that there should be found men indifferent to the loss of their being and to the danger of an eternity of misery. They are completely different with respect to everything else: they fear the slightest things, they see them before they appear, they feel them; and the same man who spends so many days and nights in rage and despair over the loss of a position or for some imaginary slight to his honour, it is that very man even who knows without worry and without emotion that he is going to lose everything at his death. It is a monstrous thing to see in the same heart and at the same time this strange sensitivity about the smallest things, this strange insensitivity about the greatest things. It is an incomprehensible bewitchment, a supernatural sleepiness which points to some almighty force as its cause." Berdyaev met in Russia, Germany and France many of the most important writers and thinkers of his time, but he confessed that he felt a real intellectual kinship only with Shestov, "...with whom my friendship has grown stronger and deeper since the Kiev and Moscow days, and he is the only person with whom I could speak about matters that are of the greatest importance to us both". The writings of Dostoevsky, Berdyaev and Shestov taken together should be considered a Summa Theologica of free Russian religious thought.

Berdyaev, also born in Kiev, was eight years younger than Shestov. They met at various times throughout their lives, became friends and both lived in Paris as exiles from Russia beginning in the early 1920s until their deaths, Shestov in 1938, Berdyaev in 1948. Berdyaev lived in Kiev for a time in a grand magnificent house at the top of a great hill. Down below the hill was an area of Kiev inhabited by merchants. It may be the area where Shestov's family lived. His father was a well educated and successful Russian Jew and we can be sure that Shestov faced personal and cultural problems with his identity as did other educated Jews of the period from Russia and from other European countries. In his writings about Heinrich Heine, a Jew who was a famous German poet, it pleased Shestov that Heine was a clever independent man who lived freely in Paris supported by a wealthy family member. Shestov was also pleased that Heine was so free spiritually and so open to all religious and intellectual influences that no one could tell whether or not he believed in God. Heine and Shestov were Jews with free spirits who were open to all European cultural influences rather than only Jewish influences. Heine started a relationship with a French girl who sold flowers his first day in Paris. Shestov married a Russian girl in Rome at the age of thirty-six who was not Jewish. He was forced to keep her background secret from his father who would have been outraged that his son had not married a Jewish girl. Shestov lived as a young man in cities all over Europe and we can be sure that he lived like Heinrich Heine as a clever independent open-minded Jew financed also by his family's wealth. Many European Jews of Shestov's time assimilated so fully the cultures of their native European countries that they abandoned influences from Jewish religion. Shestov's philosophical perspective was paradoxically powerfully anti-philosophical and he asserted that truth should be sought in the Jewish Bible. His free and independent way of life may have caused him difficulties with traditional Jewish practices but he visited Palestine and lectured there in the 1930s and abandoning Judaism as one source for his thought was out of the question. In fact, just as Berdyaev was a Martin Luther of Russian Orthodox Christianity, Lev Shestov was a Martin Luther of Judaism because his personal permanent war against rational knowledge reveals a new revolutionary religious practice possible for all humanity and especially for devout Jews. For an escape from the world of rational human knowledge is at least one step towards the world of God.

Shestov tried to assimilate all cultures ancient and modern. He knew at least four foreign languages, German, French, Ancient Greek and Latin. As an independent man like Berdyaev, he did from time to time lecture at universities in Russia and France but avoided like Berdyaev taking refuge in a career as a college professor. He studied for a doctorate in law from a Moscow university but did not receive it because his thesis was judged too revolutionary. He still could have practiced law but it did not interest him. Like Berdyaev he had no regular profession or job. He did work for a time putting his father's business in order but the main thing he did all his life was read and study all the great works of writers and philosophers from all periods of European history back to the ancient world. He and Berdyaev quote and react to so many writers from various times that it would require several pages to list them. Berdyaev in his autobiography mentions over two hundred writers. The lives of the two are an advertisement for a genuine education: read everything and think of everything as freely as possible all through your life and dare to let your voice speak truths only when you have eaten and digested all the truths of men who lived in your time or before.

Certainties about anything in life were problematic for Shestov because the evidence of our eyes is that life itself is full of uncertainties. Everything in life tends away from uncertainty and towards equilibrium. No one wants to be uncertain about anything. Our reason is incapable of relating to uncertainty. When our being feels certain about anything, our reason tells us it is real and the certainty that we feel because of reason's support proves that whatever is real is rational. It is not just Hegel's Absolute Spirit developing in history that takes some real form that is also rational. We individually in our development hour by hour, day by day, are establishing our own reality as secure and certain whenever we act in a way that seems real because we discover along with its reality its rationality. We desire not just certainty. We desire absolute certainty. We make ourselves absolutely real spirits when we live absolutely rationally. But this certainty, this equilibrium, this personal reality that is also rational is for Shestov an illusion. Dostoevsky's Underground Man acts irrationally on purpose and *reason does not abandon him.* Reason remains calmly in its regular place in his mind watching his irrational behavior indifferently. He goes in a tavern with the irrational hope that he can get someone to throw him out a window and reason goes right along with him in its regular place in his mind as usual and as usual not feeling anything at all. If the Underground Man's irrationality succeeded and he had gotten himself thrown out a window, reason would have flown right along with him through the air totally unafraid and without feeling. Whatever is real is rational but whatever is irrational is also real except that reason will not relate to it at all. A madman, an insane person, is "out of his mind" only in the sense that his emotions are going berserk and are out of his control but the reasoning capacity of his mind does not change at all. He is insane but he can think rationally. It is simply that rational thought wants nothing to do with his present plight. It can not help him. He is way out there in the blue coping with a new totally uncertain reality that does not relate to his reason even slightly. This abnormal insane condition of our being that carries along an indifferent reason with it proves to Shestov that our reason is *always* indifferent to us and that when we proclaim that something we experience is real *because* it is rational we are guilty ourselves of betraying the fundamental nature of our own being.

"Man does not dare or has no power," writes Shestov, "to think in the categories in which he lives, and is forced to live in those categories in which he thinks." He might have added that when he lives where he thinks his being is sacrificing itself to the indifferent reason in his mind. If we prethink some action and act it out our being remains real but it expresses itself in a radically diminished state. Shestov wants to know why we are compelled to live diminished by reason which falsely convinces us that it is necessary for us to feel we are real when we are perfectly capable of feeling real without it. Of course he is not asking us to throw away reason and to run out of our houses and go crazy in the streets. We do not harm ourselves if we think only in the categories where we live. But he does ask us to accept some form of craziness as a possibility because reason is a false and indifferent guide to the real. "Whatever is real is rational" is but one of many laws and theorems our reason uses to construct the knowledge we use not just in everyday practical actions but more importantly in the knowledge philosophers, scientists and theologians use to construct the truths and beliefs we are forced to accept and that reach to the foundations of our minds and our souls.

Shestov has nothing positive to tell us. He is heart and

soul against what is positive in us. It pleased him greatly when he wrote about the great Russian writer Chekhov that he always wrote about the concrete, exact, finite acts of his characters and that his creativity became intense and inspired the less they were positive and the more they were forced to deal with uncertainties and negativities. One of Chekhov's characters lives and suffers as a victim of so many chance negativities that when he is about to die it is revealed that he does not want to be immortal. Shestov explains that Tolstoy's depressing and negative stories he wrote towards the end of his long life, stories like *The Death Of Ivan Ilyich,* opened up Russian literature to the publication of the negative realism of writers like Chekhov. Shestov, Chekhov and Tolstoy in his last period had a passion for finding reality in the concrete and the finite and the three had the spiritual freedom to face boldly negativity in humans at irrational and fearful moments. Even Hegel's reason had to have negative moments in its development before it could again become positive. Job was one of Shestov's heroes, Job who cursed against positive-minded men who tried to comfort him. Abraham was another of his heroes, Abraham who abandoned all human thoughts as sources of truth and had faith only in God.

Shestov teaches us that we cannot trust reason and he describes the plight of a character in one of Tolstoy's last stories that proves that he understood that reason in some circumstances reveals itself as detached and useless. In *Master and Servant* Tolstoy places Brekhounov and his servant during a journey in a solitary region suddenly in a violent, overwhelming snow storm. "Even when it appears clearly," Shestov writes, "that the master and the servant have lost their way and that they must pass the night buried under snow, Brekhounov cannot admit that his reason, that his talents which have already so many times drawn him out of the most difficult situations, can betray him this time." During the night, he is awakened from sleep and Shestov writes, "His heart begins beating so strong, so rapidly...He feels an unreasonable terror, strong, overwhelming. 'What to do? What to do?' A question that a man always asks who finds himself in a difficult situation...but it seems this time completely absurd. Up till now this question always contained elements for his answer. In every case, it was asked seeing in advance the possibility of an answer. But this time it's not like that at all. The question excludes every possibility of an answer: there is nothing to do." Brekhounov is a strong and fearless man. He always succeeded in the past making his way to riches against every adversary, even those more powerful than he. But now he is in a terrible situation. "The adversary," Shestov writes, "was formidable and — this was the most troubling thing about it — perfectly invisible. Against what can he aim his punches? Against whom can he defend himself? Brekhounov's reason cannot admit that such a thing is possible."

Covered by snow, for the first time in his life he takes refuge in dreams. He boasts to himself about his successes and takes pleasure remembering his beautiful situation in society. But fear creeps into his being as he thinks of the past and interrupts his dream. Whatever effort he makes to remind himself of his past successful operations, of his money, of his riches, "fear little by little takes possession of his soul". Reason helps us when we are constructing a positive life for ourselves but when the living construction starts coming apart because of circumstances we cannot control, reason is no help. Brekhounov makes a last desperate effort to save himself. He abandons his servant who is asleep and freezing to death and goes off with the horse. His reason tells him to do it. But the reason that always guided him well now betrays him. Without noticing it, he continually changes direction. Everything becomes dreadful and he trembles less from cold than from fear, from a fear completely absurd, irrational. All the objects around him take on a fantastic silouette. Shestov writes, "He finds himself placed suddenly in conditions so contrary to his positive and reasonable nature that everything appears to him stupid, absurd...". Finally, "The last chance of safety disappears, terror invades and dominates his soul. The explications which up until this experience used to chase away his fears and doubts are now powerless and no longer pacify them….He has already gone past the fatal limit, he is adrift, far from solid earth, from the order that rules there, from its laws and its well-established methods for the search for truth."

Brekounov has reached a place where all of us at some time will arrive because of some kind of absurd circumstances. In our postmodern world, scientific psychology will step up and help us when irrational fears take over us and reason abandons us. We will be calmed down by drugs. We will be counseled. Psychology believes there is no soul and all our experiences come from different areas of our brain and so forth. Postmodern psychology agrees with Shestov: logic, reason rule our souls but they disagree passionately regarding the solution necessary when the soul goes adrift. Psychology uses scientific reason and knowledge to cure a soul and Shestov uses faith. Here is his solution to Brekounhov's problem with his soul and to our problems with our souls:

"The beginning of all knowledge is fear. When a man,

before he turns to God, begins to question: But what kind of God is this, and does He correspond to the exalted idea about the Supreme Being that I have made up for myself? — he repeats anew the sin of Adam, even though he imagines that in this way he is realizing his freedom. He is testing God by means of that 'knowledge' which the fruits of the forbidden tree have brought him, without even suspecting that his fear, that all his apprehensions, signify of themselves the loss of freedom. The free man is not afraid, he fears nothing; the free man does not ask, does not look around. That is why his relationship to God is expressed not in knowledge but in faith. Faith is that freedom which the Creator breathed into man along with life. And the existential philosophy — in opposition to the speculative — no longer seeks knowledge and does not see in knowledge the final and only path to truth. For this philosophy knowledge itself is transformed into a problem, becomes problematic. And in that moment when it becomes problematic, it loses its power over man... For God nothing is impossible: truths as well as reality are in His hands. Human destinies are decided on Job's balances, not on the balances of speculation."

3

Shestov writes in his book on the Danish existential writer Kierkegaard: "That which we call 'understanding' is like an enormous stone, fallen from God knows where, which has crushed and flattened our consciousness, beaten it down to the two-dimensional plane of an illusory hall-existence, and weakened our powers of thought. We can only 'accept' — we are not yet able to challenge, we are convinced that 'challenging' only spoils and corrupts human thought; Job, Abraham, and the Psalmist, in our opinion, think badly. But for existential philosophy, the greatest defect in our thinking is its loss of the ability to 'challenge', because it has thus forfeited the one dimension that alone is able to guide it to the truth."

Shestov discovered the writings of Kierkegaard late in life in the 1930s. He was well-known in the Scandanavian countries and was translated into German, but the Dane was unknown in Russia. Shestov found him to be very close in his point-of-view to himself and to Dostoevsky and he became the source of one of his last books, *Kierkegaard and Existential Philosophy*. Kierkegaard, Dostoevsky and Berdyaev were allies of Shestov against the reliance on objectivity as the source of truth. Shestov writes, "The very qualities which theoretical philosophy considers to be to its particular credit — its objectivity, its lack of passion — are seen by Kierkegaard as its greatest deficiency, its basic shortcoming. 'Men,' Kierkegaard says, 'have become too objective to attain eternal happiness: for eternal happiness consists precisely of a passionate and infinite personal concern. And they renounce this in order to become objective: objectivity robs their souls of passion and 'infinite personal concern.' The unlimited power of 'objectivity' seems to Kierkegaard unnaturally strange, mysterious, and enigmatic. And here is something to ponder, even though not one of the innumerable extollers of objectivity has ever pondered it, has ever posed the question of whence and when this power came to objectivity, and why the 'infinitely passionate concern' of living man and living Gods should have yielded to objectivity, which is indifferent to all and certainly has no concern for anything. At times one might even think that the philosophers who glorify objectivity and place all of creation in its clutches are, seemingly without knowing it, using the Kierkegaardian method of indirect communication; it is as if they were asking themselves: how much longer are the people to be scourged? The people are long-suffering, however; the people will endure everything, even objectivity."

The concession, the slavery, the resignation of most philosophers for almost three thousand years in the face of reason and its demands that they be objective, that only the rational is real, is the central theme opposed in Shestov's writings. From Anaximeter through Plato and Socrates, through Aristotle, through Plotinus, through some Christian philosophers of the early church (Shestov knows Saint Augustine's writings thoroughly enough to except him from this category) and of the Middle Ages with their reliance on Aristotle's scientific rationalism, through Descartes and Spinoza, through Hume, Kant and Hegel, through phenomenologists in modern times like Husserel, through existentialists in the 20th century like Sartre and Heidigger, Shestov finds always the same poison at the root of their thought. To be true, what they write must be, as in Descartes' language, *clare et distincte*, to be true it must be objective, it must be clear and distinct, it must be rational, it must be acceptable to the same reason that governs science and mathematics. Any thoughts not modeled by the rational mind cannot be true. Shestov had strong personal positive feelings for the Jewish philosopher Spinoza. He found inconsistencies in some sections of his writings and discovered there Spinoza's feelings for God. But Shestov, against his own positive feelings towards Spinoza, a fellow Jew writing in an European language, wrote emphatically that Spinoza's commitment to rationality killed God. Spinoza killed his feelings for God and instead submitted to reason, resigned himself to it, renounced the irrational feelings in his soul and killed God. Shestov often cites a quote from Spinoza that proves he sacrificed his natural feelings in order to understand. Spinoza wrote that it was necessary *non ridere, non lugere, neque detestari, sed intelligere*, not to laugh, not to weep, nor to pray for deliverance but to understand. To understand is to understand rationally, only rationally. Otherwise you do not understand. Otherwise you can only bang your head against the wall like the Underground Man of Dostoevsky.

Shestov's book on Kierkegaard was his last battle against our objective knowledge after a life-long fight. About the time he wrote it, he also wrote an essay against Berdyaev. He considered Berdyaev at bottom a gnostic, that is, although he was deeply spiritual and against objective knowledge as the source of truth, he had elements at least in his thought about God based on rational knowledge. Shestov claimed that Berdyaev like the German idealists based their writings on the German mystic Jacob Boehme who believed that freedom existed prior to the existence of God and independently of God. Berdyaev accepts this meonic freedom based in non-being but Shestov rejects it as a freedom that never existed. "Before the face of the Creator there are no laws, no 'you ought,' no compulsion; all chains fall away from man, and sins cease to exist. Before the face of the Creator there revives in man the authentic freedom created by God, that freedom which is boundless possibility limited by nothing — like the freedom of God Himself. When and only when man finds genuine freedom are all apprehensions and fears, and especially those fears before Nothingness ... revealed as the result of gnosis, of knowledge, and, therefore, as that terrible fall into sin about which the first chapters of the Book of Genesis tell."

As regards Nothingness, which is so important in the existential philosophy of Sartre and for him is the element in human being that condemns us to be free, Shestov gives his view in such a beautifully structured statement that we should take it as his final word about God and freedom and at the same time his refutation of the freedom of both Berdyaev and Sartre. He writes in his book on Kierkegaard:

"Everything that is not created is for that reason deprived of grace, frustrated and consequently pledged to an illusory existence. Everything that has been 'liberated' from God hands itself over to the power of nothingness. 'Dependence' with respect to God is freedom with respect to nothingness which, precisely because it is not created, sucks like a vampire the blood of everything living."

4

Every work of Lev Shestov contains again and again his negative views of reason and knowledge. We must now look to the source where he finds evidence that knowledge led to the fall of man. Does the story of Adam and Eve in Genesis make sense? Does Shestov's interpretation of the story make sense? Shestov has rolled the dice. He has bet everything on one bold gamble. It is that we are all living in an abnormal state of being. We automatically give up the freedom that leads to dependence only on God and transform the nothingness that surrounds and threatens our being into dependence on reason which assures us that everything we do under its command is real.

Shestov writes about the fall of man in his introduction to *Kierkegaard and Existential Philosophy*: "The Nothingness that the tempter showed to the first man awoke in him fear of the all-powerful will, that nothing limits, of the Creator, and seeking to protect himself against God, Adam rushed towards knowledge, towards eternal and uncreated truths. And in this respect, nothing has changed: we are afraid of God; it's in knowledge, in consciousness that we see our salvation." But for existential philosophy, for Shestov and thinkers like Dostoevsky and Kierkegaard, "Sin is not in being, it is not in what left from the hands of the Creator. Sin, vice, deficiency are in our 'knowledge'….And this 'knowledge' flattened, crushed man's consciousness by introducing it to the level of limited possibilities which now determine for his consciousness his earthly and eternal destiny." For Shestov the opposite of sin is faith in God and it was by giving up the power of faith that God had created in him that caused Adam's fall. But, at least for Christians, faith is not the only religious virtue. The three virtues are faith, hope and charity. "Charity" is an unfortunate translation to English of the Latin *"Caritas"*. *"Caritas"* is the translation to Latin of the New Testament Greek "*αγάπη*", "love", so that *"caritas dei"* means "love of God" and is synonymous with *"gratia dei"*, "the grace of God". Charity is too often understood as giving money to the poor, giving other kinds of assistance, or being kind in the sense of "having charity" towards others. As a Christian virtue it means grace, and grace for Christians can mean only an unmerited assistance from God by an entrance into the soul of divine love. Charity, grace, grace from God, and the losses of grace suffered by Adam and Eve as the result of abandoning God for knowledge point us towards a better way to understand the fall than Shestov's explanation of the fall as the result of Adam giving up faith and abandoning God because of fear of God's "all-powerful will, that nothing limits".

Shestov found In Dostoevsky's short story, *The Dream of a Ridiculous Man,* published in 1877 four years before his death, direct evidence that Dostoevsky accepted as true the fall of Adam and Eve from grace because of knowledge. In Shestov's opinion, the ridiculous man "saw in a dream what the Bible relates. He dreamed that he was among men who had not yet tasted the fruits of the tree of the knowledge of good and evil, who did not yet know shame, who did not possess science and did not know and wish to judge." He writes in the previous paragraph that he considered that the truth the ridiculous man discovered in his dream is "not at all new, is only the most ancient truth, that it is almost as old as the world, for it was revealed to man on the day following creation. It was revealed, was written in the book of books and, immediately after, forgotten. You will guess of course that I have in mind the story of original sin." But Shestov's belief that man fell because he gave up faith in God and lost his freedom by exchanging it for knowledge is not complete because it does not take into account the presence of grace in the Garden of Eden along with freedom and the loss of both. Dostoevsky's short story is remarkable because he actually creates by the genius of his description a Christ-like love existing among all the people in the paradise of his dream, that is, a grace, a presence of divine love, that is natural to their life and a grace that by implication must have been present in the Garden of Evil as told in the Bible. Shestov, a Russian Jew, has a mind and spirit completely open to Christianity. He knows well Isaiah, the Psalmist, Saint-Paul, Saint Augustine and other great Christians like Pascal. But grace somehow passes him by or at least does not influence his thought significantly. He does not know it intimately. He is heart and soul with Dostoevsky's man from the underground but he is just as far removed from grace as he. He misses the key dichotomy between grace and knowledge. He writes that, "Paradisal ignorance is in no way poorer than fallen man's knowledge; it is qualitatively different and infinitely richer than all our learning…" But does he understand that if "paradisal ignorance" is "infinitely richer than all our learning" this can only be true because life in God's paradise is "infinitely richer" because man's heart is continually full of grace which is God's divine love? He does not understand that with grace there is no need for our human knowledge at all. Because he does not know the transforming power of grace, he also does not understand that the ridiculous man in Dostoevsky's story is changed in his soul by the Christ-like love he discovered among the people he met in his dream. His soul is transformed by grace.

We should not be surprised that the hero of *The Dream of a Ridiculous Man*, written three or four years before *The Brothers Karamazov,* tells us in the very first line, "I am a ridiculous man", and uses the word ridiculous over and over again and again in his second paragraph to describe his nature during the previous years of his life. The other word he uses to describe himself is "absurd". His being is ridiculous and absurd because from birth and up to his present adult years he feels nothing permanent and fixed within him. He is ridiculous but so is Raskolnikov ridiculous using his reason to guide him to the absurd objective of murdering a woman for no reason. So is Mr. Golyadkin ridiculous discovering another Mr. Golyadkin. The man from the underground is not only ridiculous and absurd but shouts at us that he actively seeks such a condition willfully in his fight against a world enslaved by the rational logic of two-plus-two-makes-four. Dostoevsky is passionately for freedom, for groundlessness. He is not afraid to express groundlessness because he felt after receiving his "second pair of eyes" that at the bottom of his soul there was no ground and that it was ridiculous to be forced by society to act as though there was ground. Four years after publishing *The Dream of a Ridiculous Man*, and one year after publishing *The Brothers Karamazov*, he was buried before a huge crowd of his fellow Russians in Saint Petersburg as a Russian national hero. If you judge what is at the bottom of the Russian soul without including freedom or groundlessne, your judgement itself becomes ridiculous and absurd. Dostoevsky became a national hero because his words explore so truthfully the Russian soul. He knew it and the Russians knew he knew it.

His hero, his ridiculous man, admits he was ridiculous as a child, as a schoolboy, as a college student and finally "the full conviction came during the last year somehow suddenly. I suddenly felt that it would make no difference to me whether the world existed or there was nothing anywhere". In other words, the world within him seems so ridiculous that finally the whole exterior world seems ridiculous too. Nothing matters neither himself nor anything nor anyone else. Yet this ridiculous man has a strange dream and discovers the truth. He is empty but this truth, a truth reached by experiencing grace, changes him. Before his ridiculousness made him feel angry at other people. But now, " I'm no longer angry, now they are all dear to me, and even when they laugh at me — then, too, they are even somehow especially dear to me. I would laugh with them — not really at myself, but for love of them — if it weren't so sad for me to look at them. Sad because they don't know the truth, and I do know the truth.

Ah, how hard it is to be the only one who knows the truth! But they won't understand that. No, they won't understand it." His truth will not be understood but at the end of his story he tells us nonetheless exactly what his truth is. In his dream he has visited paradise on earth where humans love one another and live at peace without rational knowledge in harmony with all animals and nature. Life is in harmony naturally because love is everywhere and he, a visitor possessing human knowledge, corrupts the harmony by teaching the inhabitants to lie. The lie changes everything. They learn to make distinctions and begin to see contradictions. Contradictions between one another that they become conscious of through the visitor's introduction of knowledge among them destroys the harmony and makes the people he visits become just like ourselves on our earth. The ridiculous man, the visitor from our earth, corrupts them with knowledge and then tries unsuccessfully to save them by restoring love. He fails but when he wakes up from his dream he is changed positively and knows the truth: "A dream? What is a dream? And is our life not a dream? I'll say more: let it never, let it never come true, and let there be no paradise (that I can understand!) — well, but I will preach all the same. And yet it's so simple: in one day, in one hour — it could all be set up at once! The main thing is — love others as yourself, that's the main thing, and it's everything, there's no need for anything else at all: it will immediately be discovered how to set things up. And yet this is merely an old truth, repeated and read a billion times, but still it has never taken root! 'The consciousness of life is higher than life, the knowledge of the laws of happiness is higher than happiness' — that is what must be fought! And I will. If only everyone wants it, everything can be set up at once."

When Dostoevsky wrote the story in the 1870s a few years before his death he was not perhaps in a position as a famous man, a public figure, a magazine and newspaper writer and editor, to come right out and admit that he accepted the story in Genesis of the fall of man through knowledge as true and even profoundly true. But he did come out and write in his story of the dream of a ridiculous man the truth, " 'The consciousness of life is higher than life, the knowledge of the laws of happiness is higher than happiness' — that is what must be fought!" Consciousness of life that becomes higher than life, knowledge of the laws of happiness that is more important than happiness itself — these are the enemies. This is direct confirmation by Dostoevsky that Shestov will be correct in claiming that man lost paradise and gained nothing in return except knowledge, that he gained not life but "the consciousness of life" which "is higher than life", that he ended up not with happiness but with the "knowledge of the laws of happiness that is more important than happiness itself." But Dostoevsky does more than simply repeat the story of the fall of man. His artistic genius makes us live the fall of our parents from paradise, their fall from universal love and universal harmony among all creatures to universal discord and contradictions. But the grace the ridiculous man found in his dream of paradise transformed him. When he awoke, he decides to live only to try to communicate this grace in his soul to others. This is the grace that somehow passed by Shestov. He does not understand that the ridiculous man has been transformed, that he has discovered in his soul the secret treasure that was in Sonya's soul and that he now believes should and could be in the soul of all humanity. Shestov reads the end of Dostoevsky's story as a betrayal by the ridiculous man of what he discovered in paradise in his dream. This proves by Shestov's mistake that he missed the supreme importance of grace in understanding the reason for Adam and Eve's fall from grace in paradise as well as the fall in the paradise Dostoevsky created in his dream.

Shestov writes about the ending of the story, "But what is extraordinary… is the end of *The Dream of a Ridiculous Man*. The hero of the story has given up suicide now that the truth has been revealed to him: 'But now I want to live, I want to live! I raised my arms and called upon eternal truth; no I did not call upon it, I cried tears. An enthusiasm, an overwhelming enthusiasm, transported all my being. Yes, to live and teach! I decided immediately to expand this teaching and to consecrate my whole life to it. I am going to teach, I want to teach; but what? The truth, for I saw it, saw it with my own eyes, saw it in all its glory'."

But Shestov judges that if he teaches the truth then he turns the truth he discovered existentially beyond the range of knowledge into a regular knowledge available universally to everyone. He believes that this is a betrayal of what he discovered but he judges incorrectly because the truth the ridiculous man will try to teach is that he has been transformed by grace from an empty soul to a soul now full of love. Here is Shestov's judgement, "To teach the truth. 'I am going to teach the truth!' , that is, I am going to make a gift of it to common consciousness, which, before accepting it, will certainly demand that it submit itself to laws. Do you understand what that means? He betrayed the eternal truth that was revealed to him and sold it to his mortal enemy. In a dream he says he corrupted the pure people living in paradise. Now he hurries towards men to accomplish, fully conscious, the same crime which had already horrified him in his dream." Shestov's judgement is correct but only if grace does not exist as a reality.

Does grace exist? Did the ridiculous man experience grace in his dream of paradise? Dostoevsky knew, every Christian knows and all Christians have known for hundreds of years that the fall of Adam and Eve was a fall from grace. They fell from grace by eating the forbidden fruit. In paradise before their fall they were full of grace, but it is extremely difficult to genuinely express what the condition of grace was like. Dostoevsky avoids using the word grace but does try passionately to express it. The existence of grace has been unfortunately the kind of truth universally recognized as a common reality acceptable universally that Shestov detested. But Dostoevsky will have nothing to do in his short story with grace as an idea. He expresses its reality among the people he visits as love.

His genius carries him beyond mere words like grace and love to the reality of what God's paradise must have been like before the fall of our ancient parents. Here is Dostoevsky's description of the experience that transformed the being of the ridiculous man:

"Suddenly, as if quite imperceptibly, I came to stand on this other earth, in the bright light of a sunny day, lovely as paradise. I was standing, it seems, on one of those islands which on our earth make up the Greek archipelago, or somewhere on the coast of the mainland adjacent to that archipelago. Oh, everything was exactly as with us, but seemed everywhere to radiate some festivity and a great, holy, and finally attained triumph. The gentle emerald sea splashed softly against the shores and kissed them with love — plain, visible, almost conscious. Tall, beautiful trees stood in all the luxury of their flowering, and their numberless leaves, I was convinced, greeted me with their soft, gentle sound, as if uttering words of love. The grass glittered with bright, fragrant flowers. Flocks of birds flew about in the air and, fearless of me, landed on my shoulders and arms, joyfully beating me with their dear, fluttering wings. And finally I got to see and know the people of that happy earth. They came to me themselves, they surrounded me, kissed me. Children of the sun, children of their sun — oh, how beautiful they were! Never on earth have I seen such beauty in man. Maybe only in our children, in their first years, can one find a remote, though faint, glimmer of that beauty. The eyes of these happy people shone with clear brightness. Their faces radiated reason and a sort of consciousness fulfilled to the point of serenity, yet they were mirthful faces; a childlike joy sounded in the words and voices of these people. Oh, at once, with the first glance at their faces, I understood everything, everything! This was the earth undefiled by the fall, the people who lived on it had not sinned, they lived in the same paradise in which, according to the legends of all mankind, our fallen forefathers lived, with the only difference that the whole earth here was everywhere one and the same paradise. These people, laughing joyfully, crowded around me and caressed me; they took me with them and each of them wished to set me at ease. Oh, they didn't ask me about anything, but it seemed to me as if they already knew everything, and wished quickly to drive the torment from my face... well, let it be only a dream! But the feeling of love from these innocent and beautiful people remained in me ever after, and I feel that their love pours upon me from there even now. I saw them myself, I knew them and was convinced, I loved them, I suffered for them afterward. Oh I at once understood, even then, that in many ways I would never understand them; to me, a modern Russian progressive and vile Petersburger, it seemed insoluble, for instance, that they, while knowing so much, did not have our science. But I soon realized that their knowledge was fulfilled and nourished by different insights than on our earth, and that their aspirations were also quite different. They did not wish for anything and were at peace, they did not aspire to a knowledge of life, as we do, because their life was fulfilled. But their knowledge was deeper and loftier than our science; for our science seeks to explain what life is, it aspires to comprehend it, in order to teach others to live; but they know how to live even without science, and I understood that, but I could not understand their knowledge. They pointed out their trees to me, and I could not understand the extent of the love with which they looked at them: as if they were talking with creatures of their own kind. And you know, perhaps I wouldn't be mistaken if I said that they did talk to them! Yes, they had found their language, and I'm convinced that the trees understood them."

No one except Dante has written a better description of Paradise and Dostoevsky did it without using the word grace. But what Shestov missed in the story that is more important than whether or not he understood that Dostoevsky was describing grace is the transforming power of grace. The truth the ridiculous man is eager to teach once back in our world is that grace transformed his being and made him a new being. And since he was mysteriously transformed by personally connecting with people in paradise living full of divine love, he realizes that this divine love, grace, now living in him can be communicated by him personally, man to man, man to woman, on his earth. The existence of grace in Adam can not in itself explain his fall but his fall was a fall from grace. Our knowledge that grace is divine love poured into a soul by God that transforms a soul and creates a new being, as the ridiculous man experienced, and also our knowledge that grace can be transferred personally from one being to another creating by the power of divine love new being again and again in a long chain of being throughout the history of the Christian church can help us explain the mystery of the holy trinity. The creation of man as told in Genesis is triune. It is not just the creation of one man, Adam. Adam is created full of grace and is connected directly to the being of God. But just as God transfers personally grace from his being to Adam when as the Bible says he "breathed into his nostrils the breath of life; and man became a living soul", Adam in turn transfers his grace, the grace that created him as "a living soul", to another being, Eve, creating another new being, another "living soul". This fundamental power of grace to go beyond itself and actually create a new being in another making the other person a new person is not revealed directly in Genesis. Eve is said to be created from Adam's rib but at least what is revealed is that she was born from something in Adam's being. The trinity is present in the story of the creation of the first man and woman in Genesis. We have to first gain directly divine knowledge of the trinity itself in order to make its application to Adam and Eve clearer. If the trinity helps us explain their fall from grace by abandoning God for knowledge, it will help prove Shestov's claim that knowledge, uncreated regular earthly and human knowledge, caused the fall of man.

Grace is an experience in the heart of a love so unusual and perfect that we immediately believe it must be of divine origin. It immediately tells us it does not come from us. That is enough to make it a great mystery but there is another aspect to it that makes it even more mysterious. The strange love that does not come from us makes us not only feel love but also love whatever is the source of the love whom we do not doubt is God. How can I love God with a love that does not originate in me and yet is love I have coming from myself for God? It means that God is able not only to love us but also to create love for himself in us. This means his love for me is not only love for me but also in some mysterious way a creation of me. His love makes me feel not only that I am a person but a divine person and if scientific and rational logic teach anything true, it is certain that they teach me that I am not divine. Grace reveals that God's love is by its very essence creative. He both loves and creates the being he loves who in turn is unable to do anything with the love born in him except love his creator. And here we find a new third mystery. The love for God the newly created being feels does not give the new being a sense that his love enslaves him to his creator. It is a love freely given and freely returned to the giver that freely binds two beings together who are both free to break the bonds of their union. This total freedom in the experience means that it is a power in God that both loves and creates and frees a being able in itself neither to love, to create or to be free.

If God only forced us to love him it would not be love and we would not feel it as love but merely as some alien force. He must not simply force a being to love. He must also create a being with a being capable of experiencing his love and he must also simultaneously create a loving being capable of loving him and also to stop loving him. A real relationship with any other must create both the love and another being in the other and it can only be accomplished together with the will to totally free the other not to love its creator in return. Something like this does happen between two humans who love. It is not the divine love of grace but it is a love that like grace creates love in the beloved. I am before the other and I love. The other somehow at some time also feels a love originating in me taking birth in her. If my love is strong and true, it overwhelms me and confuses me because it is a mystery how it could have arisen in me. But it is there and it is there for certain because I feel no longer alone and I seem already joined in love with another. All individualism is suddenly gone. It is now about two persons and these two somehow share the same love which makes them one person or at least perhaps will make them one. Where does the love come from that I see appear in the eyes of the beloved that was not there before? I feel I am a different being because of love and my love rising in the heart of the other creates a new being in her. It is in this sense that we should understand the statement in Scripture that God created man in his image. I am a human image of a divine God because I can create love for myself in another being where originally there was no love. But the love that arises from God's grace does not desire to express itself by union with another body. It brings with it no sense that there is anything to do. It is a joining. It comes complete. It feels eternal. It is God and I and that is all. It is precise and limitless. I need to do nothing. Human love has a person for its object that it must unite with because the relationship that develops is not eternal and true but only personal and mortal. Human love inevitably becomes desire. It crucifies itself by driving one of the members of one body like a nail into a body powerless to do anything but receive it passively.

God's love is so full and so true and so eternal that the being his love creates must also love with a love that does not come from him and yet is also as full and as true and as eternal as God's love. Saint Francis de Sales wrote that the love in the Holy Trinity between God the father and God the son is reciprocal. This can not be true. It would mean the son existed before the father's love created him and it would mean he not only existed apart from God but also that he was capable also of a divine love originating in himself. The only possible explanation of the trinity is that God's love itself in and of itself creates another being loved with a love whose very nature returns the same love experienced as now belonging to the son to the father freely in one eternal upsurge that joins the two eternally as one person although two. And since the first person creating the second person is together with the second person now one, a new third person with the spirit created by the union of the first and second person has been created, the Holy Spirit.

It is this divine knowledge of the trinity when applied to the story of Adam and Eve in Genesis that proves Shestov's belief that human knowledge caused their fall. If God can eternally create love in a son that does not come from his son but nonetheless returns eternally and freely back to him creating one person, there is every reason to believe that God can perform the same miracle in a human man and that some writer divinely inspired can record it and relate it in writings adapted to his time and to his habit of language using an unscientific knowledge of the universe. We do not have to accept his science but we must accept his divine knowledge because we ourselves through God's grace have been given the same knowledge.

Adam or some man somewhere at some time was full of grace that came from God. It was the one and only supreme divine grace from God that also created God's son as a loving being because God's love always creates a being that freely loves him without the being being the source of the love. So a man, a human man, was full of grace. The whole inner life of his being was grace. Divine love and grace and life were all the same thing in his being. God created a human man with a totally new being just as he still today gives us the clear sense when he grants us grace that he creates us anew. His newly created man had feelings that were triune and one for they were simultaneously grace, love and freedom, the freedom that Shestov writes was lost because of knowledge. But God created man without knowledge. He did not know. He did not possess what we postmodern humans possess. He did not know anything. He did not know the love he felt was love. He did not know he loved only by the grace of God. He did not even know he was alive and free. He had no need to know anything and he did not know that he even had the possibility of knowing anything.

We all know what knowledge is. Every scientist knows what it is. God of course also knew and he knew that the new being he created in a man with a body could also possibly know because he was alive in a universe of millions of bodies separated and unrelated to one another. Knowledge is based on separation. The separation of all bodies creates in the mind the ability to see and make distinctions. Distinctions allow us to say this is good and this is not good. Knowledge is a process, a dead process, of distinguishing between separate bodies of any size and quality in any location and creating in the mind mental relationships between them when in reality they have no relationship since they are separated. Separation between bodies also creates violence and evil and new separations and in turn also requires the use of knowledge to try to create some kind of order out of chaos. God understood the risk. He created divine being in a body and that being would remain free and good and eternal as long as it did not know anything. But it was a body among countless other bodies. God gave his new being only the knowledge that once he began using his eyes to make distinctions between himself and other bodies he would know scientifically his condition as a body in his mind and this would cause a sudden shift from his divine feelings of love and grace and freedom to something in himself that has nothing to do with his three attributes joined together. He would discover the truth that his three attributes that made him himself were in reality not caused by himself and that he was merely a body like other bodies subject to death.

God gave divine being to only one human being. However this new kind of being in turn had the capacity because it was divine-human to love and create another being by creating in the other a power to love that it did not previously possess. One being, a man made divine by the power of God, loved and created another being from a power in his being that did not originate in himself and just as the union of the Father and the Son created simultaneously the Holy Spirit, the second person of the new manifestation of the trinity created divine being in a human woman making her by a transference of God's grace through the first divine-human man a holy spirit. Of course Scripture says Eve was created using Adam's rib and we are all creatures of knowledge and therefore free to enjoy a sophisticated laugh coming from our minds, minds which we have made supreme and crammed with information that has nothing to do with our souls. A rib! God created a woman from Adam's rib! Please stop laughing for a minute and ask yourself if you have ever loved a woman, really loved her. You create her. Yes, you do. You fill her old being with a new being newly alive. She loves because the look in your eyes full of love gleams into her soul a passion that sets her soul on fire. Laugh at Adam if you wish, but the man who wrote about him describes him full of "the breath of life" that God breathed into him, a breath that must have been full of love and grace since it was divine. A rib is a good enough symbol in a transfer of divine love from the heart of a divine-human to the heart of a human woman making her a divine-human. A man's rib is at least close to a man's heart, closer than the rational part of a man's mind that creates nothing divinely good.

The Adam and Eve story is the trinity in action among men. A man had a love in himself so divine that it created another man, called now a woman. He gave the grace from God that was in him to another human being and created that being anew just as God's grace had already created him, the second person of the divine-human trinity, anew. The bible says very clearly that men existed before Adam. But they were not true men capable of eternal relationships with both God and other men. God "breathed into his nostrils the breath of life; and man became a living soul." This new man could not relate to other men except by loving them (like the men and women and animals in Dostoevsky's paradise) because he had nothing in his soul but love. He could not relate to them except by creating this same love in a new person's soul that came from himself and also from God to whom he was now eternally related. No one of us living in the postmodern world can deny that that was and is a possibility! But our low and fallen inability to love so divinely and so powerfully as the first man God created loved now only serves, if we dare, to reveal to us our debased nature. Our debased nature knows! We see clearly that we are separated from everyone and everything. It is our one glory, a debased glory (the oxymoron is intentional), that we are always not loving everyone and everything but always making rational distinctions between everyone and everything. The new being Adam's love created had the possibility of this debased glory too. God warned his two new divine-human beings that they should not open their eyes. They should simply live and love freely full of grace and not begin making distinctions between one another. Once they opened their eyes knowledge would reveal to them that they were not truly united in love but in reality separate objective bodies capable like all bodies that rely only on their natural power of no eternal relationship. *"Eritis scientes"* the serpent said, *"bonum et malum sicut dei"*. "You will be beings knowing good and evil like Gods." The serpent was right. He knew. He already had his eyes open. He could make rational distinctions. But let us at least state the good news in the Adam and Eve story before we come to the bad. The creation of Eve was the third movement of the trinity operating in the human world. She was created anew not by God directly but by the power of love that God had created living through his grace in Adam. God destined this his second and indirect creation of a divine-human to continue. Eve had the power as did Adam to create more and more divine-human persons endlessly and eternally, capable all of them of being united to God's divine spirit eternally, eternally related to both God and to one another in love. But neither Adam nor Eve knew this. They did not know their life was also love or that this love that they did not know as love came freely from God's divine grace. Eve opened her eyes and knew. Ever since knowledge has been a weight loaded on our human souls as though a prison warden devoted to keeping love and grace and freedom in a dungeon.

So Adam was Christ. He was a son of God made flesh. Like Christ he was not a real man like those who already existed and had nothing divine in their nature. He was an imitation of a man for the living soul that God breathed into him was divine because God's divine love of a man makes him a new divine being. The historical Christ knew he was divine because born from God's grace in the form of the Holy Spirit and sustained eternally by his father's love but Adam-Christ knew nothing. When they, both Adam and Christ, came in contact with other men they would immediately transform them and create them with a new divine being based on divine love. They would change men and make them no longer natural men but new divine-human men now become imitations of men like themselves. How could Christ's apostles have gone forth and made men give up everything within them that made them what they were if the apostles did not have a divine being implanted in them by Christ? God's grace not only makes a man a new man but also makes the new man make other men new. Eve was converted by Adam just as men and women were converted by the apostles. She loved Adam with a love that he had implanted in her. Her name was changed by the man who wrote of her divine birth from a man to a wo man because her true being came from a man. But she could not have been born knowing she was divine-human and knowing that the love she possessed was love for the simple reason that knowledge did not exist. It had no reason to exist. God knew it would be created at any moment when his two creations used the freedom that always exists joined to divine love and grace to free themselves from the divine life within them rather than to use their freedom only to implant love, divinity and freedom in others. Eve had the power to give divinity to the serpent by loving him but instead she used her freedom to relate to him only with her mind. They talked to one another rather than loving one another. They separated mentally one thing from another thing. Making distinctions between things proved to them that they themselves could become distinct from everyone and everything and not related to anything. Eve was divine and full of love and immortal only when she did not know it. She was already *sicut dea,* like a goddess, not because she was *sciens,* knowing, but because she was not *sciens*. Instead of going off like Christ's apostles to implant divinity in men she talked to a serpent which means she used her God-given freedom to talk to something in an exterior body and to something in her own body that was not soul but only a body, a thing. She opened her eyes and knew and became only a human thing. We were all of us once destined to become living bodies receiving God's love in a divine-human chain reaction going all the way back to Adam. But knowledge broke the chain. Instead of passing down to us generation after generation the divine love they received from God, our ancient grand-parents passed down to us their original sin along with the knowledge that destroyed their freedom and that Dostoevsky and Shestov believed now enslaves us.